Microsoft SharePoint 2010 Administration Cookbook

Over 90 simple but incredibly effective recipes to administer your SharePoint applications

Peter Serzo

PUBLISHING

BIRMINGHAM - MUMBAI

Microsoft SharePoint 2010 Administration Cookbook

First published: January 2011

Production Reference: 1170111

Published by Packt Publishing Ltd.
32 Lincoln Road
Olton
Birmingham, B27 6PA, UK.

ISBN 978-1-849681-08-7

www.packtpub.com

Cover Image by David Guettirrez (bilbaorocker@yahoo.co.uk)

Credits

Author
Peter Serzo

Reviewers
Marius Constantinescu

Michael Nemtsev

Ivan Wilson

Development Editor
Wilson D'souza

Technical Editor
Gaurav Datar

Indexer
Monica Ajmera Mehta

Editorial Team Leader
Gagandeep Singh

Project Team Leader
Priya Mukherji

Project Coordinator
Sneha Harkut

Proofreaders
Stephen Swaney

Kelly Hutchison

Graphics
Geetanjali Sawant

Production Coordinator
Alwin Roy

Cover Work
Alwin Roy

About the Author

Peter Serzo is an English major from Kent State, who started his technical career with EDS after finishing college. After working for 20 years as a consultant in organizations of all sizes, he is now a national speaker on SharePoint. His next challenge is to bring SharePoint to children and teach them. He has been working with SharePoint since 2003, in companies such as Microsoft, Ford, and ADP, along with many others throughout the United States.

Currently, Peter is working as a Senior SharePoint Architect for High Monkey Consulting. The name "High Monkey" refers to an old Jamaican proverb that means the higher up you go, the more responsible you must be. High Monkey takes pride in its accountability and excellence toward work, with regard to the client's needs.

I dedicate this book to my wife Stacy, for her patience, love, and support as I took much of our time to write. She is my rock. I also thank my children—Philip, Zachary, and Stefan—for their support and belief in me. I hope this book inspires them to exceed in their lives (Think Avisha!). Finally, I want to thank my Mom, for giving me a love for the written word, and my Dad, for giving me a love and appreciation for all things technical. A perfect balance. All of you are my source of inspiration and will always have my love.

About the Reviewers

With experience in commercial software development dating back to the late nineties, **Marius Constantinescu** currently works as the Lead Architect on Microsoft Solutions, for a professional IT services company based in Geneva, Switzerland.

Having worked with .NET from its very early beta stages, as well as with the SharePoint platform since 2003, Marius has played a major part in developing useful tools for large international organizations and private companies, providing consulting expertise on architectures based on .NET, SharePoint, and other related technologies.

His passion for technology has made him recipient of various prestigious awards such as "Technology Scout for 2005" and "Siemens Certified Architect" while working as the Microsoft Solution architect for Siemens. Currently his focus has shifted again to latest .NET technologies such as Silverlight, SharePoint Server, and Cloud Computing.

Marius has been working as a Technical Reviewer of .NET technologies for almost a decade, with multiple publishing houses and prestigious authors around. He has quite a few credits added to his name, including the two best sellers on ASP.NET 2.0, written by the popular author Dino Esposito, back in 2005.

Marius is also a frequent speaker in management briefings and technology conferences, and maintains a blog, available at `http://nettitude.spaces.live.com`.

I'd like to thank my fiancé, Réka K., for her immense patience and support thorough the long late nights I had to spend away, and all the weekends traded in favor of my other passion, .NET technologies.

Michael Nemtsev is a Microsoft Most Valued Professional (MVP) in SharePoint Server and has held this status since year 2009. Previously, he had held the same award in .NET/C# area since year 2005. Michael has expertise in the Enterprise Integration Platform and Collaborations areas, and is currently working as a Senior Information Management Consultant at Gen-I in Sydney, Australia.

Ivan Wilson has been working as a consultant on Microsoft technologies for the last 15 years and has been focusing on the SharePoint platform for the last seven years. He has five Microsoft Most Valued Professional (MVP) awards to his credit—winning continuously since 2006 until 2010. Originally from Ireland, he moved to Sydney, Australia in 1999. He now co-runs SharePoint Gurus, a consultancy business focused on helping organizations collaborate in a better way.

www.PacktPub.com

Support files, eBooks, discount offers, and more

You might want to visit www.PacktPub.com for support files and downloads related to your book.

Did you know that Packt offers eBook versions of every book published, with PDF and ePub files available? You can upgrade to the eBook version at www.PacktPub.com and as a print book customer, you are entitled to a discount on the eBook copy. Get in touch with us at service@packtpub.com for more details.

At www.PacktPub.com, you can also read a collection of free technical articles, sign up for a range of free newsletters and receive exclusive discounts and offers on Packt books and eBooks.

http://PacktLib.PacktPub.com

Do you need instant solutions to your IT questions? PacktLib is Packt's online digital book library. Here, you can access, read and search across Packt's entire library of books.

Why Subscribe?

- ► Fully searchable across every book published by Packt
- ► Copy & paste, print and bookmark content
- ► On demand and accessible via web browser

Free Access for Packt account holders

If you have an account with Packt at www.PacktPub.com, you can use this to access PacktLib today and view nine entirely free books. Simply use your login credentials for immediate access.

Instant Updates on New Packt Books

Get notified! Find out when new books are published by following *@PacktEnterprise* on Twitter, or the *Packt Enterprise* Facebook page.

Table of Contents

Preface

SharePoint 2010 enables businesses to set up collaboration with, and for, many types of entities (employees, vendors, customers, and so on) while integrating disparate technologies. It has proved so valuable a tool at many organizations that its growth has led it to become a mission-critical application. As SharePoint has grown through each version, it has assimilated several technologies. It now encompasses technologies such as content management, Microsoft Access, and Visio to name a few.

The administrator's challenge with SharePoint 2010 is recognizing where to perform vital tasks in a product that is as vast as it is deep. The recipes here represent common tasks that an administrator must be knowledgeable about. These are foundational tasks that, in most cases, can be combined and built upon. Features are titled so that even if the task is performed sporadically, you can look at the title and use the book as a reference guide. It is my hope that the book becomes a resource that is referenced often.

What this book covers

Chapter 1, Upgrading and Configuring SharePoint 2010, contains recipes that deal with configuring and getting SharePoint up and going. These recipes not only cover upgrading from a previous version but also contain explanations on how to create new web applications and associated components.

Chapter 2, Service Applications, covers recipes involving service applications, which is a new concept to SharePoint 2010. These recipes cover the main service applications such as managed metadata and Excel. It also covers the components of a service application, such as custom groups, that can be configured.

Chapter 3, Farm Governance, covers different items that relate to managing SharePoint 2010. These recipes will be implemented based on guidance from your organization. The recipes support the rules that govern your organization, such as how to restrict web parts or setting up a managed account.

Chapter 4, Site Administration, contains key recipes for managing the site-level components. Error pages, content types, retention policies, and records management are some of the topics that are covered.

Chapter 5, Monitoring and Reporting, covers recipes involving the different tools in SharePoint 2010 that assist the administrator in managing SharePoint. These tools are critical to knowing how the SharePoint 2010 installation operates. The recipes show how to manage the tools.

Chapter 6, Search, covers the core components within SharePoint 2010. The topics here range from how to scale out the Search components to customizing search. Search is a broad foundational topic in SharePoint and the recipes here provide a granular view into what an administrator can do.

Chapter 7, Security Administration: Users and Groups, contains recipes related to user access. The list of topics range from site collection-level access to site-level access.

Chapter 8, Content Management, is about different aspects of SharePoint 2010. These recipes range from term sets, setting up a content type hub, routing documents, to managing external content types.

Chapter 9, Social Architecture, is a new topic for SharePoint 2010. The features covered in the recipes have to do with setting up a tag cloud managing the social features for a user. The recipes give the administrator a broad range of where and how the social environment can be managed in SharePoint.

Chapter 10, Backup and Restore, is a topic that should be familiar to all administrators. The recipes here cover everything from the recycle bin to a farm backup and restore.

Chapter 11, Performance Monitoring, covers some lesser-known ways to monitor SharePoint. The recipes here introduce tools, some of which are not native to SharePoint, but the functionalities they provide assist the administrator without requiring a financial investment. The recipes show how to use these readily available tools.

What you need for this book

In order to perform the recipes within this book, a functional installation of SharePoint 2010 Standard is required. SharePoint 2010 is resource intensive on hardware. The recipes in this book have been tested using a laptop with 8 gigabytes of RAM and a 500 gigabyte hard drive. The environment includes Windows 2008 R2, with SharePoint 2010 Enterprise, using SQL Server 2008 R2 Standard. The environment has been created using a native boot virtual hard disk (VHD), which is supported by Windows Server 2008 R2.

The configuration that you choose will most likely use some type of virtualization software such as VMWare or Hyper-V. Also you can choose the native boot solution as I have done while writing this book.

The following are the core software components you will need to perform the recipes in this book:

- ▶ Windows Server 2008.
- ▶ 64-bit version of SQL Server 2008 Standard with Service Pack 1. The database engine and tools must be installed.
- ▶ SharePoint 2010 Enterprise (which comes only in 64-bit).
- ▶ Virtualization software such as VMWare or Hyper-V.
- ▶ Visual Round Trip Analyzer.

This book does not cover installation and configuration. In order to perform these tasks, refer to an online resource such as Microsoft's Technet: `http://technet.microsoft.com/en-us/sharepoint`.

Who this book is for

If you are a SharePoint Administrator looking for solutions to the many problems faced while managing SharePoint, then this book is for you. This book is written for SharePoint administrators, who are either already working on SharePoint, or have recently started working and are eager to learn more about SharePoint administration. You need to have some basic knowledge of SharePoint in order to follow the recipes in this book.

Conventions

In this book, you will find a number of styles of text that distinguish between different kinds of information. Here are some examples of these styles, and an explanation of their meaning.

Code words in text are shown as follows: "Create a site collection called `sites\ContentTypeHub`, based on the Publishing Site Template, and make yourself the owner."

A block of code is set as follows:

```
<Category    Title="Author"    Description="Use this filter to
restrict results authored by a specific author"    Type="Microsoft.
Office.Server.Search.WebControls.ManagedPropertyFilterGenerator"
MetadataThreshold="5"    NumberOfFiltersToDisplay="4"
MaxNumberOfFilters="20"
```

Any command-line input or output is written as follows:

```
Get-SPEnterpriseSearchServiceApplication
```

New terms and **important words** are shown in **bold**. Words that you see on the screen, in menus or dialog boxes for example, appear in the text like this: "Under the **Site Actions** section, click **Manage site features**."

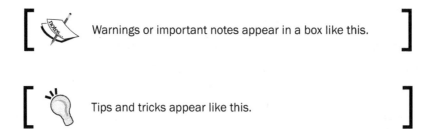

Warnings or important notes appear in a box like this.

Tips and tricks appear like this.

Reader feedback

Feedback from our readers is always welcome. Let us know what you think about this book—what you liked or may have disliked. Reader feedback is important for us to develop titles that you really get the most out of.

To send us general feedback, simply send an e-mail to feedback@packtpub.com, and mention the book title via the subject of your message.

If there is a book that you need and would like to see us publish, please send us a note in the **SUGGEST A TITLE** form on www.packtpub.com or e-mail suggest@packtpub.com.

If there is a topic that you have expertise in and you are interested in either writing or contributing to a book, see our author guide on www.packtpub.com/authors.

Customer support

Now that you are the proud owner of a Packt book, we have a number of things to help you to get the most from your purchase.

Errata

Although we have taken every care to ensure the accuracy of our content, mistakes do happen. If you find a mistake in one of our books—maybe a mistake in the text or the code—we would be grateful if you would report this to us. By doing so, you can save other readers from frustration and help us improve subsequent versions of this book. If you find any errata, please report them by visiting http://www.packtpub.com/support, selecting your book, clicking on the errata submission form link, and entering the details of your errata. Once your errata are verified, your submission will be accepted and the errata will be uploaded on our website, or added to any list of existing errata, under the Errata section of that title. Any existing errata can be viewed by selecting your title from http://www.packtpub.com/support.

Piracy

Piracy of copyright material on the Internet is an ongoing problem across all media. At Packt, we take the protection of our copyright and licenses very seriously. If you come across any illegal copies of our works, in any form, on the Internet, please provide us with the location address or website name immediately so that we can pursue a remedy.

Please contact us at copyright@packtpub.com with a link to the suspected pirated material.

We appreciate your help in protecting our authors, and our ability to bring you valuable content.

Questions

You can contact us at questions@packtpub.com if you are having a problem with any aspect of the book, and we will do our best to address it.

1
Upgrading and Configuring SharePoint 2010

In this chapter, we will cover:

- ▶ Checking current installation upgradeability
- ▶ Upgrading MOSS 2007 to SharePoint 2010
- ▶ Upgrading with minimal downtime
- ▶ Visual upgrade
- ▶ Creating and associating content databases to a specific web application and site collection
- ▶ Configuring a content database
- ▶ Creating an Alternate Access Mapping (AAM)
- ▶ Patching (compatibility boundaries)

Introduction

SharePoint 2010 requires 64-bit architecture on the servers, with a minimum of 8 gigabytes of RAM. The result of this requirement is that there will be installations upgrading their 32-bit architecture and then upgrading/migrating their sites.

Upgrading SharePoint 2010 is optimally a one time job. In reality, this is not always the case as there may be business reasons one web application is upgraded and another is left in MOSS 2007. This could be due to software integration with SharePoint, components that are not ready for SharePoint 2010, or a segment of users that need time before upgrading to SharePoint 2007.

SharePoint 2010 has been architected with the capability to migrate sites methodically. With this in mind, every recipe in this chapter approaches the upgrade from the viewpoint of iterative tasks after an upgrade. This means that a majority of the tasks can be performed several times against different web applications.

Every recipe here (except the first one) should be performed and understood by the administrator of the SharePoint 2010 farm. There are many new items in SharePoint 2010 that will become common tasks; some more than others depending on the size of your environment.

One of the best new tools that should be in your arsenal is PowerShell. The recipes in this section outline the commands you will need. However, after reviewing and trying these recipes, look at scripting your tasks with PowerShell. This will enable you to become a more effective and proactive IT Professional.

Checking current installation upgradeability

In order to upgrade to SharePoint 2010 from your current Windows SharePoint Services 3.0 (WSS) or Microsoft Office SharePoint Server 2007 (MOSS) implementation, you need to plan your new infrastructure carefully. When thinking about planning your new architecture, take into account the logical design and the physical design of the new SharePoint 2010 installation.

Issues need to be identified, resolved, and requirements need to be met. Issues can range from addressing 32-bit architecture to custom site definitions. These items need to be resolved before being able to update to SharePoint 2010.

Begin your planning by identifying and documenting your current infrastructure. Review the hardware, WSS/MOSS configurations, and potential customizations.

A typical farm installation will have multiple servers with diverse roles: web front ends, applications servers, database servers, among others. Extrapolating from there, an installation can have multiple content databases, web applications, site collections, Shared Service Providers, to name a few of the components.

In order to manage your infrastructure and plan for the SharePoint 2010 upgrade, Microsoft has provided organizations with a tool called preupgradecheck. This tool is shipped as part of MOSS Service Pack 2. As long as this service pack is applied, the tool is available.

This tool documents the current installation, checks your MOSS/WSS installation against SharePoint 2010 requirements, and applies best practice rules identifying areas of concern.

Getting ready

In order to execute this tool, the WSS 3.0/MOSS 2007 installation must have the Office 2007 Service Pack 2 installed. This tool is native to the SharePoint installation and an extension of the `stsadm` command.

You must be a member of the Farm Administrators SharePoint Group, with administrator permissions on the server.

How to do it...

1. Click **Start** and **Run...** on the web front-end server.
2. Type in **cmd** and press *Enter*.
3. Navigate to `c:\Program Files\Common Files\Microsoft Shared\web server extensions\12\BIN`. This can be achieved with the help of the CD (Change Directory) command.
4. Type the following in the command prompt:

   ```
   stsadm -o preupgradecheck
   ```

   You should see a report that looks similar to the following screenshot:

How it works...

The pre-upgrade application leverages rules that can be found in the following two files: `OssPreUpgradeCheck.xml` and `WssPreUpgradeCheck.xml`.

These files were created in `12\CONFIG\PreUpgradeCheck` when the Microsoft Office SharePoint 2007 Service Pack 2 was installed. Refer to the next screenshot:

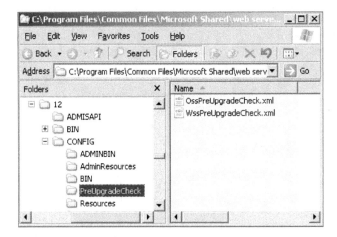

In the command prompt window shown in step 4 of the previous section, a summary of the operations is shown. The objects marked with the colors yellow and red must be addressed. The farm will not get upgraded until objects in red color are addressed.

As you can see from the preceding screenshot, an HTML file is created in the `12\Logs` folder, which contains the information the pre-upgrade application produced. The first part of the report produces important information as shown in the following screenshot:

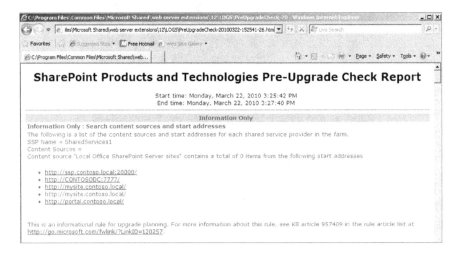

Other information collected includes the SharePoint version, supported upgrade types, along with information on your servers, including roles, amount of data, number of web applications, site collections, and number of servers.

The rest of the HTML report lists the checks that were done and any issues that were found. If an issue is found, the report will include a description on fixing the issue or a link to a Microsoft Knowledge Base article that corresponds to the issue.

There's more...

The pre-upgrade application performs read-only operations against the database. No changes are made to your SharePoint installation. This means you can run the application multiple times and there is no adverse effect on your SharePoint installation. As you resolve issues, it is advisable that you rerun the pre-upgrade application.

More info

Using the `preupgradecheck rule files` parameter, you can create your own custom rules to identify items that are specific to your installation.

Upgrading MOSS 2007 to SharePoint 2010

There are two approaches to upgrading your WSS 3.0/MOSS 2007 farm to SharePoint 2010. They are:

▸ **In-place upgrade**: This is where you will upgrade your current installation on the hardware it currently resides on.

▸ **Database attach upgrade**: To perform this type of upgrade, you must have a new SharePoint 2010 farm up and running. You will take the content databases from the MOSS 2007 farm, attach them to the new farm, and upgrade them.

The latter method of upgrading your MOSS 2007 farm is the preferred method and the one that this recipe outlines. It has many advantages over the in-place upgrade method. Some of these advantages are:

▸ It leverages backup and restore through SQL Server Management Studio. SharePoint IT Administrators should already be familiar and comfortable using these tools.

▸ The `addcontentdb stsadm` command should already be familiar to many SharePoint Administrators. It creates a new content database or as in the case outlined in this recipe, adds a database that needs to be upgraded. Attaching a database reduces the downtime of your SharePoint installation. This reduces the pain your customers will feel and enhances the success and acceptance of your upgrade.

▸ You can perform the upgrade in an iterative fashion, or even in parallel. The in-place upgrade is a one-way, don't-look-back upgrade.

- You can have granular control over the steps of your upgrade. You control what gets upgraded, when, and how. This allows for flexibility, which is the key to a successful upgrade.

SharePoint 2010 has a completely different Services architecture as compared to MOSS 2007 Shared Services. This new architecture must be planned carefully and implemented according to the organization's needs. By doing a database attach, your farm will correctly consume the new architecture as architected.

Getting ready

The `preupgradecheck` should already have been run on your current installation and any issues should have been resolved. Be sure to identify the content database that is being upgraded.

A new SharePoint Server 2010 farm must be set up and configured using a web application.

You must have access to SQL Management Studio with the ability to create databases.

How to do it...

1. Log in to the WSS 3.0/MOSS 2007 database server.
2. Open Microsoft SQL Server Management Studio and connect to the database server hosting the SharePoint content database.
3. In the **Object Explorer**, click on the folder named `Databases`.
4. Find the identified content database. By default, this is called `wss_content_{guid}`. The {guid} is a unique number generated when the database is created but it may not be present.
5. Right-click on the content database and select **Tasks | Back Up**. A screen similar to the following screenshot appears:

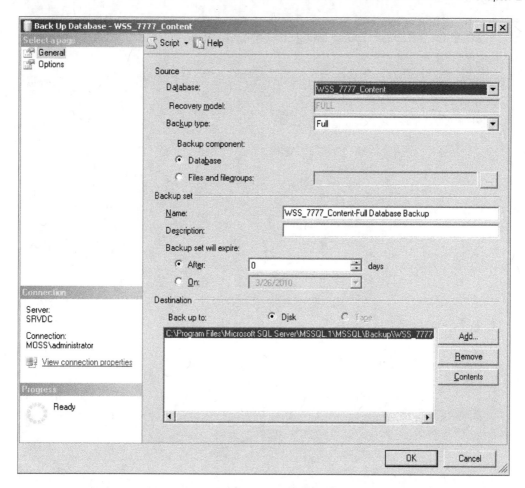

6. Ensure **Backup type** is set to **Full**. Also the **Name** and **Destination** field should be populated correctly.

7. Click **OK**. The file should be backed up successfully after a period of time.

8. Ensure the backup is accessible to the SharePoint 2010 database server. If the SQL Server is physically not on the same server as SharePoint, copy the backup to the destination server where it is accessible.

9. Through SQL Server Management Studio, connect to the SQL Server instance where the SharePoint 2010 databases are installed.

10. In the **Object Explorer** window, right-click **Databases**. Navigate and click on **Restore Database**. The following screenshot appears and must be filled with appropriate values:

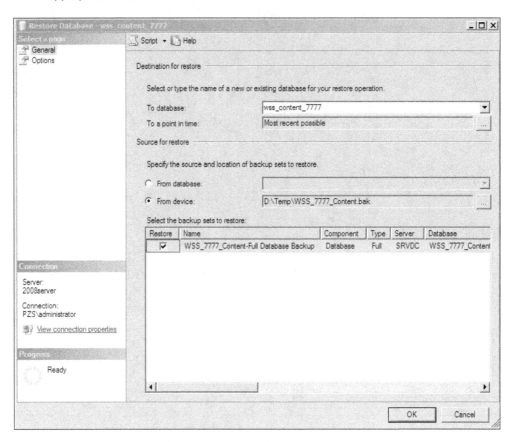

- ❑ Fill in the **To Database** textbox.
- ❑ Choose the backup file in the **From Device** option. Check the **Restore** option under the **Select the backup sets to restore** option. Click **OK**.

11. After the content database is successfully restored, it must be added to the SharePoint 2010 Web Application using `addcontentdb`, which is an argument to the `stsadm` command.

12. Open a command window. Make sure to run it as administrator when you open it. If you right-click on the command prompt, there is an option provided to **Run as Administrator**.

13. Type in the following command:

```
stsadm -o addcontentdb -url <url> -databasename <database name>
```

Here is the screenshot I get when I run this command:

```
c:\Program Files\Common Files\Microsoft Shared\Web Server Extensions\14\BIN>stsa
dm -o addcontentdb -url http://2008server:7777 -databasename wss_content_7777

100.00%
Operation completed successfully.
```

14. When the operation finishes successfully, navigate to the SharePoint 2010 Central Administration site.
15. Click the **Application Management** option. Under **Site Collections**, click the **Change Site Collection Administrators** option.
16. Ensure that there is a valid site collection administrator.

Navigate to the new site.

How it works...

Steps 1 through 7 showed how to take a backup of the content database that was being upgraded. Step 8 is copying the physical file that is created from the backup to the new server. Using file storage and rights, the file may not have to be copied. The important part of this process is that the new SQL instance for SharePoint 2010 has access to this file.

Steps 9 through 11 performed a restore to put the backup file into the new SQL database instance.

Steps 12 through 14 ran the command that performs the physical upgrade of the file. An upgrade of the content database is nothing more than schema changes, table changes, and stored procedure changes. It also adds the content database to the specified web application.

In steps 15 and 16, we, as Farm Administrators, ensured that the Site Collection Administrator from MOSS 2007 is still a valid account in the now upgraded SharePoint 2010 farm.

The database attach method is the least intrusive upgrade when it comes to your SharePoint Farms. For SharePoint 2010, upgrading with addcontentdb can be done only through the stsadm command; its functionality is not found in the Central Administration User Interface.

Finally, there is a parameter called preserveolduserexperience in the addcontentdb command. This is an optional parameter and set to true by default. When the site is upgraded to SharePoint 2010, it will contain the same look as it did in MOSS 2007. If you want the site to use the new SharePoint 2010 look, then ensure that you use this parameter and set it to false.

Depending on the farm architecture, you may have more than one content database per web application. In a case such as this, it is more efficient to upgrade both simultaneously. This is accomplished by doing multiple attaches in parallel. Instead of using the addcontentdb command, use PowerShell and the Mount-SPContentDatabase command.

There's more...

Before adding the content database to the web application, there is an additional tool that has been added via SharePoint's PowerShell commands. This tool confirms that the new web application has all the necessary components to support the upgrade. It functions by comparing the database you are about to attach/upgrade against the web application you wish to attach.

The command is Test-SPContentDatabase.

1. Click **Start | All Programs**. Select **Microsoft SharePoint 2010 Products** and then **SharePoint 2010 Management Shell**. Refer to the following screenshot:

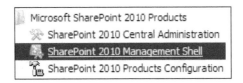

2. At the command prompt, type in the following command:

```
test-spcontentdatabase –name <database name> webapplication <url>
```

This command will produce a report in the window that can be piped to a file through PowerShell. The report will identify issues such as missing site definitions, features, or assemblies. The benefit of this command is that it works read-only against your web application so that it can be run iteratively. As you resolve issues, you can rerun the command.

Keep this command as part of the IT Professional toolkit. It is very useful to scan and identify issues against WSS 3.0/MOSS 2007 and SharePoint 2010 databases.

More info—further upgrade info

After the upgrade and migration is complete, you will see a successful or unsuccessful indicator in the command prompt. However, the best place to view the status of your upgrade is in Central Administration. This is especially true if there are parallel upgrades happening.

1. Open the SharePoint 2010 Central Administration site.
2. Click **Upgrade and Migration.**
3. Click **Check Upgrade Status**. There will be a screenshot similar to the following:

Status	Server	Start	Last Updated	Errors	Warnings
Succeeded	**2008SERVER**	**3/27/2010 3:55:24 AM**	**3/27/2010 3:57:18 AM**	0	0
Failed	2008SERVER	3/26/2010 9:37:19 PM	3/26/2010 9:39:54 PM	18	269

Selected upgrade session details

Status	Succeeded
Server	2008SERVER
Start	3/27/2010 3:55:24 AM
Last Updated	3/27/2010 3:57:18 AM
Errors	0
Warnings	0
Starting object	SPContentDatabase Name=wss_content_7777
Current object	
Current action	
Step within the action	0
Total steps in this action	0
Elapsed Time	00:01:54
Percentage completed	100.00%
Process Name	STSADM
Thread Id	2220
Process Id	7736
Command Line	stsadm -o addcontentdb -url http://2008server:7777 -databasename wss_content_7777
Log File	C:\Program Files\Common Files\Microsoft Shared\Web Server Extensions\14\LOGS\Upgrade-20100327-035524-652.log
Remedy	

As can be seen in the preceding screenshot, there were two upgrades that took place. One failed and one succeeded. One of the items on the report is the location of the log file, which shows detailed information about the failures.

There is also a custom error log file created that is necessary to look at when there are errors in the upgrade.

Also, there is a category named **Remedy**. In here is located a hyperlink to a possible resolution for the issues found.

More info—errors when upgrading

There are times when the upgrade fails. If that occurs, you may see a screen similar to the following:

```
c:\Program Files\Common Files\Microsoft Shared\Web Server Extensions\14\BIN>stsa
dm -o addcontentdb -url http://2008server:7777 -databasename portalcontent

100.00%
Upgrade completed with errors.  Review the upgrade log file located in C:\Progra
m Files\Common Files\Microsoft Shared\Web Server Extensions\14\LOGS\Upgrade-2010
0326-213719-150.log.  The number of errors and warnings is listed at the end of
the upgrade log file.
```

When this occurs, you are directed to the log file in order to determine what the issue is and how to go about resolving it.

Upgrading with minimal downtime

The SharePoint farm administrator must minimize the impact of upgrading a MOSS 2007 farm to SharePoint 2010. How long this process takes is dependent on the size of the installation.

MOSS 2007 SP2 installed a new capability that allows an administrator to set the content database to read-only. The result of this is that users can only read from the database and cannot perform any write operation.

The advantage of this when doing an upgrade is that users can continue using the MOSS 2007 farm while the data is being upgraded on the SharePoint 2010 farm.

This recipe shows how to set a database as read-only.

Getting ready

WSS 3.0/MOSS 2007 installation must have the Office 2007 Service Pack 2 installed.

How to do it...

1. Open Microsoft SQL Server Management Studio.
2. Log in to the WSS 3.0/MOSS 2007 database server.
3. In the **Object Explorer**, click the folder named `Databases`.
4. Find the correct content database. By default, this is called `wss_content_{guid}`.
5. Right-click on correct content database, and select **Properties**.
6. Under the **Options** selection, scroll down until the main window with the **State** section is visible. Refer to the next screenshot:

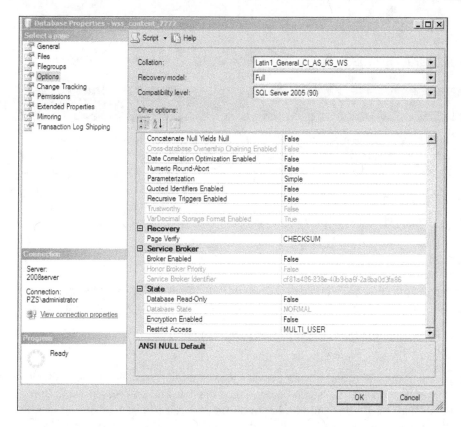

7. Change the **Database Read-Only** property to `True` from the existing value of `False`.

8. Click **OK**.

How it works...

Once the content database is read-only, no changes can be saved to the database. The WSS 3.0/MOSS 2007 site is still available to query information to the entire user population. The database can now be backed up with confidence in the integrity of the data state.

The database can be copied to the new SharePoint 2010 SQL Server and upgraded as shown in the previous recipe. When the new environment is ready to go, perform an **Alternate Access Mapping** (**AAM**) redirect to route users to the new environment and detach the database in SharePoint 2007.

This is referred to in Microsoft Technet as a Hybrid upgrade.

See also

▸   *Upgrading MOSS 2007 to SharePoint 2010.*

Visual upgrade

When upgrading your site to SharePoint 2010 from MOSS 2007, there is a significant difference in the user interface (UI). SharePoint 2010 has a new master page that includes new and changed components that must be taken into account when designing the UI. They are:

▸   The ribbon

▸   Social features such as being able to tag

▸   Disappearance of My Links

▸   Changes to `core.css`

These factors may present a challenge when porting the site's look and feel to SharePoint 2010. The business may not have the time and bandwidth to accommodate the changes.

As seen in the upgrade from recipe 2, there is an option to preserve the MOSS 2007 UI in SharePoint 2010.

Then, as the organization is ready for the new look and feel, it can be applied at a site level or at a site collection level. This can be done as a preview and then rolled back. Or the SharePoint 2010 UI can be committed permanently to your site.

Getting ready

The person doing this must be a site collection administrator or site owner, and the upgrade must have been applied with the MOSS 2007 look preserved.

How to do it...

1.   Navigate to the site where the SharePoint 2010 UI will be applied.

2.   Click **Site Actions** and then **Visual Upgrade** as seen in the following screenshot:

3. A screen is presented with three options:

    ❑ **Display the Previous SharePoint user interface**

    ❑ **Preview the new SharePoint user interface** (it can be rolled back if there is a problem)

    ❑ **Use the new SharePoint user interface** (this is permanent)

    Choose the **Preview...** option.

4. The site is now presented with the new SharePoint 2010 UI.

5. To roll the site back or commit the site to the new UI, click **Site actions | Visual Upgrade**. Choose either of the options: **Display the Previous SharePoint user interface** or **Use the new SharePoint user interface**.

How it works...

SharePoint 2010 ships with the MOSS 2007 master pages, application pages, and CSS files. It provides the facility to convert those deprecated layouts to the new UI through the visual upgrade.

This makes sure organizations do not have to make the visual leap to SharePoint 2010 all at one time. It can be phased in and tested properly, ensuring all the UI assets and UI changes function correctly.

There's more...

The visual upgrade can also be done at the site collection level through the administration page. This will allow the site collection administrator to apply the SharePoint 2010 UI to all sites under the Site Collection or hide the visual upgrade from the site owners.

The caveat to doing an upgrade to all sites is there is no preview. Any issues that result in the new UI must be dealt with immediately. There is no changing back to the MOSS 2007 pages.

The steps to achieve this are:

1. Click **Site Actions**, **Site Settings**.
2. Under the **Site Collection Administration**, there is an option for visual upgrade. The screenshot is the screen we get:

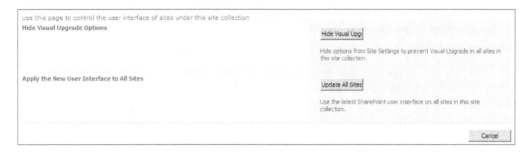

Choose either of the following options: **Hide Visual Upgrade** or **Upgrade All Sites**.

More info—changing UI version with PowerShell

There are times when a visual upgrade must be rolled back after it has been committed. This may be due to issues with the ribbon or CSS styling. In any event, the upgrade has been made and now the company wants to roll it back.

Using PowerShell, it is possible to change the look back to MOSS 2007. Use the following snippet to change the look back for a single site:

```
$web = Get-SPWeb http://server/site
$web.UIVersion = 3
$web.UIVersionConfigurationEnabled = $true
$web.Update()
```

Creating and associating content databases to a specific web application and site collection

A web application is not limited to using a single content database. SharePoint allows you to associate many content databases to a web application. One of the reasons to do this could be based on the size of the content database. If the content database is larger than 200 gigabytes, it makes more sense to distribute this content across two content databases.

A different consideration is factoring the type of data that is being housed in the content database. If there is a marketing site that contains media files such as photos and video, it may be desirable to create a content database just for this site collection data. Another example is housing all legal data into one content database/site collection for a litigation department.

Finally, a major benefit of doing this is disaster recovery. Knowing where your data is, and how it is structured, will allow you to implement a disaster recovery strategy that is efficient, effective, and flexible.

The data that is created is not the same, that is, we have various kinds of data. Data has different properties and may even have different backup and restore service level agreements. However, multiple content databases may be connected to one web application.

This recipe will show how to create multiple content databases to one web application and apply the appropriate site collection to the corresponding content database.

Getting ready

Ensure that you are a member of the Farm Administrators SharePoint group on the computer accessing the Central Administration site. You must have the correct permissions to create a database (typically dbcreator and sysadmin).

How to do it...

1. Open the **Central Administration** screen. Under **Application Management** in the **Databases** section, click **Manage Content Databases**.

2. At the top of the resultant page is the **Add a content database** option. Click the option and the following screenshot will be displayed:

Warning: this page is not encrypted for secure communication. User names, passwords, and any other information will be sent in clear text. For more information, contact your administrator.

Web Application

Select a web application.

Web Application: **http://2008server:7777/** ▾

Database Name and Authentication

Use of the default database server and database name is recommended for most cases. Refer to the administrator's guide for advanced scenarios where specifying database information is required. To change the database server and database name, use the Set-SPUsageApplication PowerShell cmdlet from the SharePoint Management Console.

Use of Windows authentication is strongly recommended. To use SQL authentication, specify the credentials which will be used to connect to the database.

Database Server

    2008Server

Database Name

    WSS_Content_5c8f9e20efe547558827e

Database authentication

    ⦿ Windows authentication (recommended)
    ○ SQL authentication
       Account

       Password

Failover Server

You can choose to associate a content database with a specific failover server that is used in conjuction with SQL Server database mirroring.

Failover Database Server

Search Server

Search service is provided by:
SharePoint Server Search

Database Capacity Settings

Specify capacity settings for this database.

Number of sites before a warning event is generated

    9000

Maximum number of sites that can be created in this database

    15000

[OK]   [Cancel]

3. The database name is given a GUID suffix by default. Change the database name to be relevant but use a naming convention. In the case of the preceding screen, I will change database name to `WSS_Content_Marketing`. Keep the rest of the defaults and click **OK**.

   The content database will be created and listed under **Manage Content Databases**.

4. To ensure that the site collection gets added to the proper content database, ensure that you are still under **Manage Content Databases**.

5. Click on the content database(s) you don't want the site collection to get added to.

6. Under the **Database Information** settings, set the **Database status** to **Offline.** Click **OK**. Refer to the next screenshot:

Database Information

Specify database connection settings for this content database. Use the **Database status** options to control whether or not new Site Collections can be created in the database. When the database status is set to **Ready**, the database is available for hosting new Site Collections. When the database status is set to **Offline**, no new Site Collections can be created.

Database server
2008Server

SQL Server database name
wss_content_7777

Database status
Offline ▾

Database Read-Only
No

Database authentication
Windows authentication

7. Navigate to **Application Management**, then **Site Collections**. Under this section, click **Create site collections**.

8. Fill the information for **Title**, **URL**, select a template, and include a primary site collection administrator. Click **OK**.

9. The site collection should be created and added to the appropriate content database. To check this, navigate back to the **Manage Content Databases** screen. See the example shown in the following screenshot. `WSS_content_7777` is **Stopped** (offline) and the new site has been added to `WSS_Content_Marketing`.

Database Name	Database Status	Database Read-Only	Current Number of Site Collections	Site Collection Level Warning	Maximum Number of Site Collections
wss_content_7777	Stopped	No	2	9000	15000
WSS_Content_Marketing	Started	No	3	9000	15000

10. Reverse the action from step 6 and put the content database back in Ready state.

How it works...

The first half of the procedure is self explanatory. We are creating a content database under the appropriate web application. The second half of the procedure takes the database offline. This action will ensure that the next site collection cannot be added to that database.

The action of assigning a site collection to a content database is very similar to network load balancing. The site collections are assigned quite evenly across the content databases while they are online.

There's more...

When doing a SharePoint 2010 upgrade of multiple content databases, ensure that the first content database that you add contains the root site for the associated web application. The rest of the content databases for the web application can be added in any order afterwards.

More info

There will be times when you do not want to add any more site collections to a content database. In order to accomplish this, perform the following steps:

1. In **Central Administration**, under the **Databases** section, click on the **Manage Content Databases** option.

2. Click on the database that you wish to no longer add site collections to.

3. Change the **Maximum number of site collections** settings (under **Database Capacity Settings**) to be equal to the current number of site collections.

4. Change the **Number of sites before a warning event is generated** setting to be one less that the current number of site collections.

More info

You have seen how to do this recipe through the user interface. There is a way to do the same procedure through scripting. PowerShell is the new way of scripting, but the stsadm command set is still available. Here are both methods:

- Using stsadm command:

```
stsadm -o createsiteinnewdb -url <url> -owneremail <email>
-ownerlogin <domain/name> -sitetemplate <site template> -title
<title> -databaseserver <serverdb> -databasename <dbname>
```

- Using PowerShell, we need to run the following two commands:

```
New-SPContentDatabase
```

```
New-SPSite
```

Configuring a content database

In SharePoint 2010, content databases are the heart of an organization's data. This is where all the site content information, such as documents, list data, and web part properties, is stored. By default, the content database is set up with parameters that may not be optimal to your organization.

Thankfully, these parameters can be changed and tweaked to fit your installation. It is important to note what can be changed and the ramifications of the change. In this recipe, you will be exposed to the parameters and the possible changes that can be made.

Getting ready

Ensure that you are a member of the Farm Administrators SharePoint group on the computer accessing the Central Administration site.

How to do it...

1. Open **Central Administration**. Under the **Databases** section, click **Manage Content Databases**. A listing of content databases will be shown in blue.

2. Click on the content database whose parameter you wish to change. The screen with the parameters to be changed will appear. The items that can be changed are:

   - Database Information
   - Failover Server
   - Database Capacity Settings
   - Search Server
   - Remove Content Database
   - Preferred Server for Timer Jobs

3. Make the appropriate changes and click **OK**.

How it works...

- ▶ **Database Information**: This section gives information on the status of the database. The drop-down list allows the administrator to change the database state. When a content database is taken offline, it is not available and sites cannot be created within it. Refer to the next screenshot:

Database Information

Specify database connection settings for this content database. Use the **Database status** options to control whether or not new Site Collections can be created in the database. When the database status is set to **Ready**, the database is available for hosting new Site Collections. When the database status is set to **Offline**, no new Site Collections can be created.

Database server
2008Server

SQL Server database name
wss_content_7777

Database status
Ready ▾

Database Read-Only
No

Database authentication
Windows authentication

▶ **Failover Server**: This is a new option within SharePoint 2010. Entering a server name into this box will not set up the failover server. It tells SharePoint what failover database server to utilize in the event one is needed. Refer to the following screenshot:

Failover Server	Failover Database Server
You can choose to associate a content database with a specific failover server that is used in conjunction with SQL Server database mirroring.	

▶ **Database Capacity Settings**: This section controls the number of site collections that will be created within the content database. There is a warning level, which must be at least one less than the maximum number of sites that can be created. Refer to the following screenshot:

Database Capacity Settings	Number of sites before a warning event is generated
Specify capacity settings for this database.	9000
	Maximum number of sites that can be created in this database
	15000

▶ **Search Server**: The content database will utilize a search server. Depending on your environment, there may be more than one server in this drop down.

Search Server	Select Microsoft SharePoint Foundation search server
You can choose to associate a content database with a specific server that is running the Microsoft SharePoint Foundation search service.	

▶ **Remove Content Database**: This section allows the administrator to disassociate the content database from the web application. It does not delete the content database from the SQL Server. The data is still available and untouched. Any content in the site collections, contained in the content database, will no longer be accessible. Refer to the next screenshot:

Remove Content Database	Remove content database
Use this section to remove a content database from the server farm. When you select the **Remove content database** check box and click **OK**, the database is no longer associated with this Web application. **Caution:** When you remove the content database, any sites listed in that content database are removed from the server farm, but the site data remains in the database.	

▶ **Preferred Server for Timer Jobs**: In SharePoint 2010, we can dedicate a server for timer jobs. This server would be indicated here for the content database. Refer to the following screenshot:

Preferred Server for Timer Jobs	Preferred Server for Timer Jobs
	No selection

Creating an Alternate Access Mapping (AAM)

SharePoint's repository is the content database that resides in the SQL server. These databases house all the data for an organization. Organizations may require that users outside the company have access to a subset of this data. For example, vendors may wish to see if their invoices have been paid.

Another example at a large enterprise is hourly workers may see a different subset of data than salary workers. The data all resides in the same content database.

Appropriately architecting the taxonomy and authentication lead into providing two different URLs. The end user will put in the appropriate URL and be directed to the trimmed content associated with that URL.

This is the point of AAMs. This recipe shows how to set up an AAM and the components involved.

Getting ready

Ensure that you are a member of the Farm Administrators SharePoint group on the computer accessing the Central Administration site.

There should also be an existing web application.

How to do it...

1. Open the **Central Administration** screen and click **System Settings**.
2. Under the **Farm Management** section, select the **Configure alternate access mappings** option.
3. A list of the current AAMs, associated with the web application, will be presented. This will be shown in the upper right-hand portion of the screen.
4. Click **Add Internal URLs**.

5. Fill in the data in the screen that appears. In the following screenshot, we have entered a URL as an example:

6. Click **Save**. The updated listing of AAMs will be visible.
7. Set up DNS to correctly reference the URL that was just entered.

How it works...

When the URL is entered by a user, IIS takes the page request and passes it to SharePoint. It is SharePoint's job to fulfill this request. SharePoint checks the AAM to make a decision on which web application to map the request.

There's more...

A point of confusion about AAMs is that they can be used for redirecting sites, with a completely new URL, to a custom port. For example, consider the following URL: `http://spmysite:2222`.

This URL cannot be redirected to a URL such as `http://mysite`.

If a SharePoint site is created on a port other than port 80(HTTP) or port 443(HTTPS), the port number must be supplied. AAMs deal only with the base URL for a web application.

More info

Host headers allow IIS to use a single port for multiple sites on the same machine. The result of this is that organizations do not need to use custom ports. That is why in this book, we have asked to use port 80.

See also

▶ *Extending a web application*

Patching (compatibility boundaries)

SharePoint 2010 brings a new story when it comes to applying updates. Typically when applying a service patch, there are two components that get updated: the web front end (WFE) and the database(s). When applying patches with WSS 3.0/MOSS 2007, an administrator had to start the process on one WFE, get it to a certain point, then start the patching on another server, and when the process got to a certain point, finish the patching process.

With SharePoint 2010, there is a new concept known as Compatibility Boundaries as it applies to patching. This will allow your WFEs to be at a different patch level than your database(s). The administrator can upgrade multiple SharePoint servers at the same time. The configuration wizard (PSConfigUI) handles this process itself without any manual intervention.

If you have large content databases, it can take some time to apply patches. This new approach means you can now patch the files on your SharePoint servers, but delay the updates to the databases until a more appropriate time. This is useful to quickly protect your environment against any newly discovered security vulnerabilities or resolve any non-database bugs.

In addition, Central Administration has several components where your patching level can be monitored. This recipe shows you the components within Central Administration where you should be checking for database schema versions, patch levels, and general monitoring of the patching process.

Getting ready

Ensure that you are a member of the Farm Administrators SharePoint group on the computer accessing the Central Administration site.

How to do it...

1. Open the **Central Administration** screen and click **Upgrade and Migration**.
2. Click on **Check product and patch installation** status. A report is pulled up showing all the product components from the farm.

3. There is a drop-down list at the top that allows you to select whether to look at the whole farm or only the components on a particular server. A part of the report looks like the following screenshot:

View: **Farm ▾**			
Server	Product	Version	Install Status
2008SERVER	**Microsoft SharePoint Server 2010**		**Installed**
2008SERVER	Microsoft Access Services English Language Pack	14.0.4536.1000	Installed
2008SERVER	Microsoft Access Services Server	14.0.4536.1000	Installed
2008SERVER	Microsoft Document Lifecycle Components	14.0.4536.1000	Installed
2008SERVER	Microsoft Document Lifecycle Components English Language Pack	14.0.4536.1000	Installed
2008SERVER	Microsoft Excel Mobile Viewer Components	14.0.4536.1000	Installed
2008SERVER	Microsoft Excel Services English Language Pack	14.0.4536.1000	Installed
2008SERVER	Microsoft Excel Services Web Front End Components	14.0.4536.1000	Installed
2008SERVER	Microsoft InfoPath Form Services English Language Pack	14.0.4536.1000	Installed
2008SERVER	Microsoft InfoPath Forms Services	14.0.4536.1000	Installed

4. Navigate back to **Upgrade and Migration** and select **Review database status**. A report is displayed, detailing all the databases for the Farm and their status.

SQL Instance	Database	Type	Status
2008Server	SharePoint_AdminContent_e749adc3-7592-47c7-8207-5c1e3aa39ac9	Content Database	No action required
2008Server	WSS_Content	Content Database	No action required
2008Server	wss_content_7777	Content Database	No action required
2008Server	WSS_Content_Marketing	Content Database	No action required
2008Server	Application_Registry_Service_DB_2beb313b0ab846bd9d11563dd94a0703	ApplicationRegistryServiceDatabase	No action required
2008Server	Bdc_Service_DB_3e8ca3d6bdaf4b7c9f325bbb4660d7fd	BdcServiceDatabase	No action required
2008Server	Managed Metadata Service_a402fb3eee214ac7a20f4c66e17bb44d	MetadataWebServiceDatabase	No action required
2008Server	PerformancePoint Service Application_bb7d2ab6ec1f44a5b9c678b46a5ab9e7	BIMonitoringServiceDatabase	No action required
2008Server	PZS_Config	Configuration Database	No action required
2008Server	Search_Service_Application_CrawlStoreDB_213082db0e054af8b0238ff3ab8adc04	SearchGathererDatabase	No action required
2008Server	Search_Service_Application_DB_6c7a502e57f5484ab4f86ea926d54277	SearchAdminDatabase	No action required
2008Server	Search_Service_Application_PropertyStoreDB_001b307e56d246deb2dc83b8968ca15a	SearchPropertyStoreDatabase	No action required
2008Server	Secure_Store_Service_DB_1478eac2a3044e07a21b2e2c90c1440e	SecureStoreServiceDatabase	No action required
2008Server	StateService_d6a533abb03f445abd63b0b13e928cf1	StateDatabase	No action required
2008Server	User Profile Service Application_ProfileDB_f14822ecb1bd40a6b276c4819504de18	ProfileDatabase	No action required
2008Server	User Profile Service Application_SocialDB_b3973ba1e0c8428fb4c2f1b270dafc9c	SocialDatabase	No action required
2008Server	User Profile Service Application_SyncDB_f749b7c7a91a430aa7b2279f6525022e	SynchronizationDatabase	No action required
2008Server	WebAnalyticsServiceApplication_ReportingDB_41826b72-53fc-46bb-b979-facd557e183b	WebAnalyticsWarehouseDatabase	No action required
2008Server	WebAnalyticsServiceApplication_StagingDB_840fa196-9df0-4a86-b223-103bbc8696e0	WebAnalyticsStagerDatabase	No action required
2008Server	Word Automation Services_01d406460823408a9b31c519a3d3ea5f	QueueDatabase	No action required
2008Server	WSS_Logging	SPUsageDatabase	No action required

5. Navigate to **Application management | Databases | Manage Content Databases**.

6. Click on a content database. The second section is called **Database Versioning and Upgrade**. It details the database schema versions and looks as shown in the next screenshot:

Database Versioning and Upgrade	Database Schema Versions
Use this section to check the version and upgrade status of this database. If the Current SharePoint Database Schema Version is less than the Maximum SharePoint Database Schema Version, the database should be upgraded as soon as possible.	Microsoft.SharePoint.Upgrade.SPContentDatabaseSequence Current Schema Version: 4.0.137.0, Maximum Schema Version: 4.0.137.0 Microsoft.SharePoint.Upgrade.SPContentDatabaseSequence2 Current Schema Version: 4.0.8.0, Maximum Schema Version: 4.0.8.0 Microsoft.SharePoint.Upgrade.SPContentDatabaseStoreProcedureSequence Current Schema Version: 14.0.4536.1000, Maximum Schema Version: 14.0.4536.1000 Microsoft.SharePoint.Administration.SPContentDatabase Current Schema Version: 14.0.4536.1000, Maximum Schema Version: 14.0.4536.1000

How it works...

The recipe shows three components of the patching story. Together, these components provide a comprehensive view to the administrator of the SharePoint Farm. Utilizing this information, the administrator can make informed decisions as issues are brought up, and can decide if a new patch must be applied.

The three components are:

- **Patch Status**: This shows the patch level of the servers. If there is something missing or required, it will be flagged with a hyperlink to the patch that is needed.
- **Database Status**: This is a listing of all the databases in the farm including SQL instance. With SharePoint 2010, there are many databases and they can be run in a compatibility range. Under status, there will be a message letting the administrator know what is required or what is happening.
- **Database Schema Versions**: This shows the current schema version and the maximum schema version that the database can be updated to.

There's more...

SharePoint 2010 monitors the health of your farm using a set of rules that are programmed against best practices. An administrator can review these rules and run them on demand or change their schedule. When a rule is broken, the issue is flagged and a red bar with a hyperlink to view the issues will appear on the Central Administration home page.

These are found under Central Administration, under a section called Monitoring. In that section is a **Review rule definitions** hyperlink. The rules for patch management can be found under the section **Configuration**. Refer to the following screenshot:

Category : **Configuration** (28)			
Alternate access URLs have not been configured.	Daily	Yes	No
The Application Discovery and Load Balancer Service is not running in this farm.	Hourly	Yes	No
Automatic Update setting inconsistent across farm servers.	Daily	Yes	No
Built-in accounts are used as application pool or service identities.	Weekly	Yes	No
Missing server side dependencies.	Weekly	Yes	No
Databases require upgrade or not supported.	Daily	Yes	No
Databases running in compatibility range, upgrade recommended.	Daily	Yes	No
One or more categories are configured with Verbose trace logging.	Daily	Yes	No
Outbound e-mail has not been configured.	Weekly	Yes	No
Recommended server upgrade available.	Daily	Yes	No
Product / patch installation or server upgrade required.	Daily	Yes	No

More info

PowerShell is a powerful enabler for the SharePoint Administrator. There are three commands that are applicable to this process.

- ▶ To produce a listing of all the patches on the server:

  ```
  Get-hotfix
  ```

- ▶ Return a listing of content databases and their GUIDs:

  ```
  Get-spcontentdatabase
  ```

- ▶ To upgrade the database:

  ```
  Upgrade-spcontentdatabase -id <GUID>
  ```

2
Service Applications

In this chapter, we will cover:

- ▶ Managing a service
- ▶ Creating the Secure Store
- ▶ Creating custom security for a service
- ▶ Creating a custom service application proxy group
- ▶ Managing service application associations
- ▶ Setting up Excel Services
- ▶ Setting up PerformancePoint Services
- ▶ Setting up Visio Services
- ▶ Setting up Managed Metadata Service
- ▶ Establishing a trust relationship between two farms
- ▶ Publishing a SharePoint Service
- ▶ Consuming another Farm's Service

Introduction

SharePoint 2010 introduces an overhaul of the MOSS 2007 **Shared Service Provider** (**SSP**). It is such a significant paradigm change that those who are responsible for implementing SharePoint must understand architecting to a different level.

MOSS 2007 had the SSP. The SSP encapsulated Search, Excel Calculations Services, user profiles, and the business data catalog. This is a "box" of services. This box was limited because you could not break it apart. One of the reasons it was limited was the fact that the services within affected the whole farm. If Accounting wished to use Excel Calculation Services, the whole farm was affected, even those not using it. In addition, writing an integrated custom service was out of the question.

SSPs are gone in SharePoint 2010. Microsoft has taken the SSP concept and built a new service application infrastructure that is flexible, extensible, and scalable:

> ► **Flexible**: Services can be segmented to a particular group of users providing security boundaries. They can also be consumed by a subset of groups. For instance, Accounting and Engineering could share an instance of PerformancePoint Services. Legal is unaffected and cannot consume the work the other two groups are doing.

> ► **Extensible**: Custom services can be written and "bolted" onto the existing architecture. An example of this is PowerPivot. It provides its own service that utilizes the existing architecture.

> ► **Scalable**: Services are the application layer of SharePoint. As resources are consumed, more boxes may be necessary to scale properly. The service architecture provides for this possibility.

Service applications for SharePoint 2010 can be viewed very similarly to the cable TV paradigm. With cable TV, we have a lot of channel choices and they are presented to us in packages. It becomes a decision as to what package you wish to consume. Premium content costs more and includes channels such as HBO. There is basic cable that typically includes local channels showing programs that are created at a city level; high school football team games would be an example of this.

Basic cable is comparable to the service applications in SharePoint Foundation. By paying a very little amount or nothing at times, you are able to get basic functionality such as Business Connectivity Services.

Moving up to SharePoint Standard is akin to having stations such as TBS, AMC, and so on. It is the middle tier of packages. In our scenario, this is services such as Managed Metadata and Search, which can be subscribed to via different server farms.

Applications such as Excel Services and Visio are comparable to the premium content such as HBO, as these applications come bundled only with the enterprise version of SharePoint.

There are three tenets that you must know when architecting and supporting service applications.

> ► Services included in the different versions of SharePoint

> ► Services dependent on the others

> ► Services that can be shared across farms

The following diagram summarizes the versions and some of the characteristics:

Service applications	Description	Stores data?	Cross-farm?	SharePoint Foundation 2010	SharePoint Server 2010 Standard	SharePoint Server 2010 Enterprise
Access Services	View, edit, and interact with Microsoft® Access® 2010 databases in a browser.	Cache				✓
Application Discovery & Load Balancer	Manages Services Application groups across Web Applications and does administrative tasks		✓	✓	✓	✓
Application Registry Service	Enables backward compatibility with the Business Data Catalog API	DB	✓	✓	✓	✓
Business Data Connectivity	Access line-of-business (LOB) data systems.	DB	✓	✓	✓	✓
Excel Services Application	Viewing and interact with Excel files in a browser.	Cache				✓
Managed Metadata Service	Access managed taxonomy hierarchies, keywords and social tagging infrastructure as well as Content Type publishing across site collections.	DB	✓		✓	✓
PerformancePoint	Provides the capabilities of PerformancePoint Services.	Cache				✓
Search	Crawls content, produces index partitions, and serves search queries.	DB	✓		✓	✓
Secure Store Service	Provides single sign-on authentication to access multiple applications or services.	DB	✓		✓	✓
Security Token	Authenticates objects (users) to	DB	✓	✓	✓	✓

Other products such as Office web applications, Project Server, and PowerPivot ship their own services applications.

Most service applications use their own application pool, under which their web service runs. One of the positive effects of this structure is if something goes wrong with that service, it will not affect the rest of the farm. Another positive effect is the ability to implement least privileged accounts. The factor to keep in mind when creating application pools is the amount of resources that they consume—in particular, RAM.

When installing SharePoint 2010, certain configurations are set by default using wizards. We assume no wizards in any of these recipes.

Managing a service

In order to manage a service application, the Farm Administrator or service application administrator will either administer through the Central Administration website or through PowerShell.

There is a **Manage Service Applications** page that lists all the services running on the farm that you have rights to manage. This will be clearly shown in the recipe you are about to follow.

Many services have their own administration page and in this recipe you will learn how to navigate to these and will be shown the functional processes that you can do from the ribbon. For our example, we are using the Managed Metadata Service.

Getting ready

You must have Farm Administrator privileges to the Central Administration website.

How to do it...

1. Open up the SharePoint 2010 Central Administration website.

2. Under the section titled **Application Management**, click on **Manage service applications**, which can be found under the **Service Applications** section. The following screenshot appears:

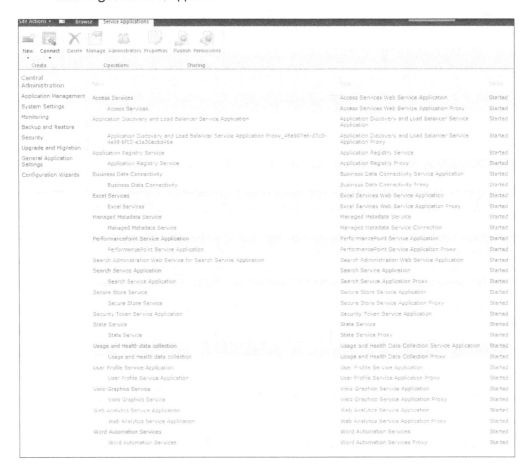

When navigating to this page for the first time, the administrator can perform several operations from the ribbon. You can create or edit an existing service application or connect to another farm's service application.

The key is to pay attention to the ribbon at the top and to the innate visual cues. Depending on what is clicked, different ribbon components will light up. This is known as being context sensitive.

3. Navigate to a Service Application's administration page by clicking on the service name. For instance, hover your cursor over the **Managed Metadata Service**, and it will be underlined as shown in the next screenshot:

Managed Metadata Service	Managed Metadata Service	Started

When you click on the service application name, the respective management page is loaded.

4. Another way to manage the components of the service is to click to the right of the service application name. The entire line item becomes highlighted in blue as seen here:

Managed Metadata Service	Managed Metadata Service	Started
Managed Metadata Service	Managed Metadata Service Connection	Started

5. Observe the ribbon. All the features are now lit up as seen in the next screenshot:

Prior to this step, the only action we could perform from the ribbon was to create a new service application or connect to a service application that has been published.

Now we can:

- **Delete** a service application.
- **Manage** a service application. This brings us to the same page that step 4 brought us.
- Assign **Administrators** to manage this service application. This is called delegation.
- View and edit the **Properties** of the service application.
- **Publish** the service application for another farm to be able to consume its services.
- Assign **Permissions** to accounts that can access the service application.

How it works...

The **Manage Service Application** page will show you all services you can manage in the farm and their status. If you do not have the rights to manage a service application, it will be security trimmed from your view.

The service application itself is listed first. Underneath it, indented, is the service application proxy that connects a consumer of this service from the web front-end to the service application.

A service application may have one, more than one, or all of the following components:

- ▶ Database(s)
- ▶ Administrative page
- ▶ Application pool
- ▶ A running physical instance

Only the services that have been installed will be listed on the page. Finally, the services that will be available depend on the version of SharePoint that is installed.

There's more...

Shared services make use of **Windows Communication Foundation** (**WCF**). As such, when the service applications are started, if you look in IIS, there is an associated web service provisioned in the virtual directory called **SharePoint Shared Services**. Expanding this directory you will see each service in the guise of a GUID. This GUID is not very helpful.

Right-click on a GUID, navigate to **Manage Application**, and then **Advanced Settings**. You will see the next screenshot:

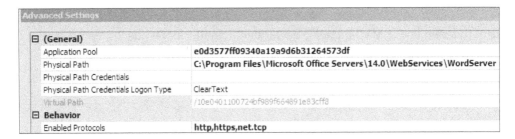

As **Physical Path**, you can see the service that is associated with the GUID. You can also see that all services reside in the `C:\Program Files\Microsoft Office Servers\14.0\WebServices\folder`.

More info

Using PowerShell, you can obtain a listing of all the farm service applications, their status, and their associated GUIDs. Using PowerShell, the command is as follows:

```
Get-spserviceinstance
```

Creating the Secure Store

The Secure Store service can be referred to as a core service because several other services require this service to be set up and configured in order to function. A part of its offering is a secure database that stores credentials associated with application IDs. These IDs are used to access content from external data sources. This is accomplished by creating unattended accounts that are stored within the Secure Store database. An example of this will be seen in an upcoming recipe with Excel Services configuration. The Secure Store will be used to house the ID that will access the data sources that the dashboards will display. These are external data sources such as SQL Server or SAP. MOSS 2007 also provided this functionality through the use of the application proxy ID. The problem with this scenario is that it does not follow the least privileged account rules.

SharePoint 2010 uses the new Secure Store and a completely separate ID from the proxy. This means now an account can be set up with only the rights it needs to access the proper data.

In this recipe, you will be shown how to set up the secure store.

Getting ready

Central Administration must be set up and you must be a Service Administrator for the Secure Store service. The Farm Administrator also has permissions to perform this action.

Create an Active Directory account, which will be configured as the identity for the application pool created for this service application.

How to do it...

1. Open up the SharePoint 2010 Central Administration website.

2. Under the section titled **Application Management**, click **Manage service applications**.

3. On the ribbon, in the top left corner, is a **New** button. Click the arrow to see all the services that can be created. Select the **Secure Store Service** option as seen in the following screenshot:

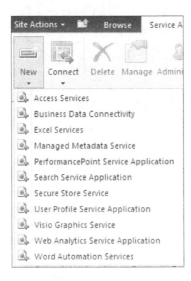

4. A form appears with the following fields to be filled in:

   ❑ **Name**: Fill in the Service Application Name.

   ❑ **Database Server**: SQL Server machine name.

   ❑ **Database Name**: The name of the Secure Store database to be created. You can modify the GUID at the end of the name.

   ❑ **Database Authentication**: Choose the Windows authentication radio button.

   ❑ **Failover Database Server**: Fill this in if you have a server configured for this operation. This will not create a failover database.

   ❑ **Application Pool**: Create a new application pool and give it an appropriate name.

   ❑ **Associate a security account**: Use **configurable** and an existing domain account that was created as part of the requirements.

□ **Audit Log**: By default, this is enabled and the textbox is populated with the default value of **30** days.

Click **OK**. The Secure Store application will be created and the page will navigate back to the listing of service applications.

5. Once the new Secure Store Application is created, click on it.

6. A key must be generated to encrypt the database. This is done based on a pass phrase. The pass phrase must be at least eight characters long and must have at least three of these four elements—uppercase characters, lowercase characters, numeric characters, and special characters. The following screenshot shows the presentation screen:

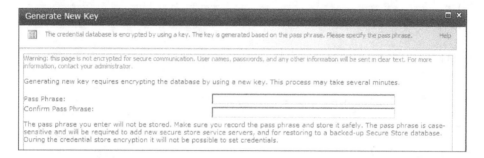

7. Click **OK** after filling in the **Pass Phrase and the Confirm Pass Phrase** textbox.

The service is now operational.

How it works...

At the heart of the Secure Store service is the Secure Store database that will contain credentials to be used for accessing external data sources. These credentials are encrypted and decrypted via the key that was generated when the pass phrase was created.

The information that is filled out in step 4 is the identity of the database, the authentication method, the application pool it uses, and a potential Failover Database Server. The failover database server would need to be set up independently as identifying a server as failover does not configure it.

There's more...

PowerShell can be used in place of the UI to create the Secure Store service application. Before creating a new Secure Store service application, ensure that the Secure Store service is running. This can be confirmed by doing the following:

1. Open **Central Administration**.
2. Click **System Settings.**
3. Click **Manage Service on Server** under the **Server** section.
4. Ensure the **Secure Store Service** says started.

Secure Store Service	Started	Stop

Using the following PowerShell command, we can create the Secure Store Service application:

```
New-spsecurestoreserviceapplication –Name $serviceapplicationname
-partionmode:<false> -sharing:$false -databaseserver $dbserveraddress
-applicationpool <apppool> -administrators <adminscommaseparated>
-auditingenabled:<true> auditlogmaxsize 30
```

Using the following PowerShell command, we can generate/refresh the key:

```
Update-spsecurestormasterkey -serviceapplicationproxy <proxy>
-passphrase <farmpassphrase>
```

```
Update-securestoreapplicationserverkey -serviceapplicationproxy <proxy>
-passphrase <farmpassphrase>
```

Using the following PowerShell command, we can get a listing of running services:

```
Get-SPServiceInstance
```

More info

The encryption key should be backed up because you may need to use it again in case you have to restore a backed up Secure Store database or if you add a new application server to the farm.

Creating custom security for a service

With the advent of the service applications and their innate standalone nature, Farm Administrators have the ability to delegate responsibility on a per service basis. No longer is the Farm Administrator the only person managing the SharePoint deployment and, as a consequence, becoming a bottleneck for the organization.

In this recipe we can see that services can be assigned to the responsible party. The Central Administration UI will show only the pages for which the Server Administrator has rights.

As an example, search is a critical component to many SharePoint 2010 installations and typically there is a Subject Matter Expert who would be the administrator of this service. Now that person can be assigned the role and that is the only search service they will have access to administer.

Getting ready

You must have Farm Administrator rights or be an administrator of the service to perform this action.

The service you choose must be started and configured.

Create an Active Directory account that will be configured as an administrator for the Service Application.

How to do it...

1. Open **Central Administration** and click the **Application Management** option.
2. The third section is **Service Applications**, click **Manage Service application**.
3. Navigate to the service on which you are going to delegate authority. You can do this by finding the Service application and clicking to the right of the name. The whole line will be highlighted as seen in the next screenshot:

| PerformancePoint Service Application | PerformancePoint Service Application | Started |

4. When the whole line is highlighted, the ribbon lights up as seen in the next screenshot:

5. Click on the button named **Administrators**. An input form will be displayed.

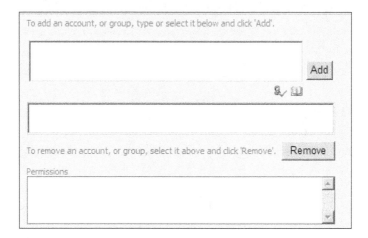

The first box is the people picker box. Here, you will type in the name of the person you wish to administrate the service application. By clicking the check icon, the system will validate the user. You can also click the book icon and use the people picker.

6. After the administrator(s) are chosen, click the **Add** button. The **Permissions** box will dynamically be populated showing the level of control.

7. Finish the process by clicking **OK** at the bottom of the form. The administrators are now assigned.

How it works...

When a domain user account is granted permissions to a service application, they are given the rights to manage the associated service. From an administrative view, this is empowering to the user and takes the responsibility from IT.

In addition, the user will be able to navigate to the **Manage Service Applications** web page, but will be granted rights to only those services for which they have permissions. The user will have access to these services through Central Administration. They will be shown a subset of the Central Administration User Interface.

The user will not see any other services, nor will they be able to manage any other services through PowerShell.

There's more...

PowerShell can be used in place of the UI to delegate administrative roles, using the following command:

```
Set-SPServiceApplicationSecurity <serviceapplication> -objectSecurity
<security>  -admin
```

Creating a custom service application proxy group

Service application proxy groups organize which service applications are consumed by a web application. To make this functionality beneficial, it is recommended to name these groups in a logical manner. In this recipe, we will create a custom name for an application proxy group.

When creating a service application, it will automatically be assigned to the default proxy group. Out of the box, there are two application proxy groups:

▶ Default

▶ Custom

It is possible to assign a service application to a custom proxy group. The benefit of creating custom proxy groups are:

▶ Greater flexibility for creating a set of services for a web application.

▶ More efficient use of resources such as hardware.

▶ A proxy group creates a service application proxy boundary. Web applications cannot consume service applications associated with a different proxy group. For instance, WebApp A is associated with proxy group #1. This group has a finance-managed metadata service . Proxy group #2 has a product-managed metadata service. In this setup, WebApp A can consume only the finance-managed metadata service and not the product-managed metadata service.

This is done through PowerShell. There is no user interface to create this component.

Getting ready

You must have local administrative permissions to the SharePoint 2010 web front-end (WFE). You must be a member of the `SharePoint_Shell_Access` database role on the configuration database. You also must be a member of the `WSS_ADMIN_WPG` local group on the chosen server.

How to do it...

1. Click the **Start** button on the WFE.

2. Under **All Programs**, navigate to the `Microsoft SharePoint 2010 Products` folder.

3. Right-click on **SharePoint 2010 Management Shell** and click **Run as Administrator**. The PowerShell console will appear. Type in the following command:

   ```
   New-spserviceapplicationproxygroup -name SAPGFinancial
   ```

4. The service application proxy group is created after submitting.

How it works...

Service application proxy groups are the ambassadors of the service application technology. They match web applications to the associated service application proxies. In this way, web applications are consuming only those service applications that they have access to.

An application proxy group can contain multiple service applications, even of the same type (for example, two instances of Excel Services). Refer to the following diagram:

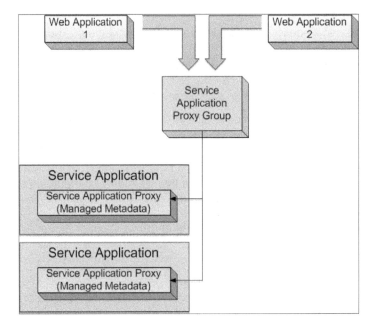

There are two web applications utilizing the same proxy group. The proxy group routes them to their service application proxy group. In this case, there are two managed metadata service applications.

There's more...

It is important to know what application proxy groups are already in the farm. Getting a listing of these groups is done through PowerShell. It may also be necessary to delete service application proxy groups that are no longer necessary. The following two PowerShell commands give you this ability:

- ▸ Listing all Service Application Proxy Groups:

  `Gget-SPServiceapplicationproxygroup`

- ▸ Remove a Service Application Proxy Group:

  `Remove-spserviceapplicationproxygroup -identity <serviceappname>`

Managing service application associations

Web applications obtain access to the content through a tiered infrastructure. The tiers are depicted in the following diagram:

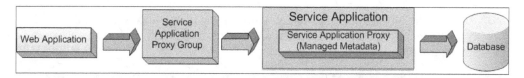

There can be multiple service application proxy groups. You can logically associate your web applications in these proxy groups. In this recipe, we will show how to modify the proxy group membership.

Getting ready

You must have Farm Administrator privileges to Central Administration.

Create an application proxy group as outlined in the preceding recipe. In our example, we have created a group called `SAPGFinancial`.

How to do it...

1. Open **Central Administration** and click **Application Management**.

2. The third section is **Service Applications**. Click the **Configure service application associations** option. You will see a screenshot similar to the following:

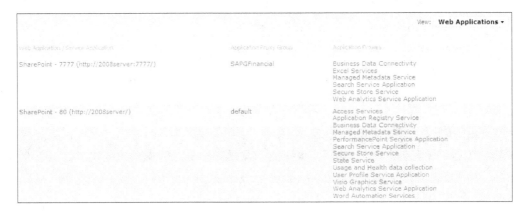

3. Click on the SAPGFinancial group option. A pop up will appear that will enable you to choose the service applications you want to associate with this application proxy group.

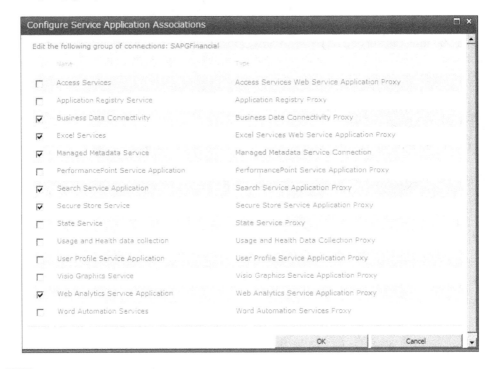

4. Choose the service applications proxies you wish to enable/disable and click **OK**.

How it works...

As seen in the previous recipe, we created a service application proxy group. Then when the web application was created, we associated it with the service application proxy group; in this case, it was `SAPGFinancial`. Initially, there were no service application proxies in this group.

Now that the web application is associated with the proxy group, it may consume the service application resources. As you can see from the preceding figures, service applications can exist in multiple application proxy groups.

However, it is important to note that a web application can be associated with only *one* application proxy group.

There's more...

You can use PowerShell to modify service applications that are associated with application proxy groups. This is powerful when scripting your environments for a seamless installation.

- Creating Service Application Association:

  ```
  Add-spserviceapplicationproxygroupmember –identity
  <serviceappproxygroup> -member <members>
  ```

- Creating Service Application Association:

  ```
  remove-spserviceapplicationproxygroupmember –identity
  <serviceappproxygroup> -member <members>
  ```

See also

▸ *Creating a Custom Service Application Proxy Group*

Setting up Excel Services

Excel Services is a standalone Service Application, giving users the ability to render their spreadsheets through SharePoint into the browser. Some of the benefits that are derived from this architecture are:

▸ Ability to delegate administration of the service to particular users. This takes the burden of management from IT down to a user level. A SharePoint group can be created for users who will administrate this service.

▸ Dedicate a server to run the service. This provides a level of adaptability and scalability as your organization's needs change.

- This gives organizations a place to collaborate and helps prevent the spread of spreadsheets in files shares.

In order to leverage this technology, you must know how to set up this service application. In this recipe, we cover the steps necessary to create an Excel Services Service Application.

Getting ready

You must have Farm Administrator privileges to Central Administration.

How to do it...

1. Open **Central Administration** and click **Application Management**.
2. The third section is **Service Applications**. Click **Manage Service applications**.
3. On the ribbon, click **New** and **Excel Services Application**.
4. You will get the following screen. Fill in the information and click **OK** when finished.

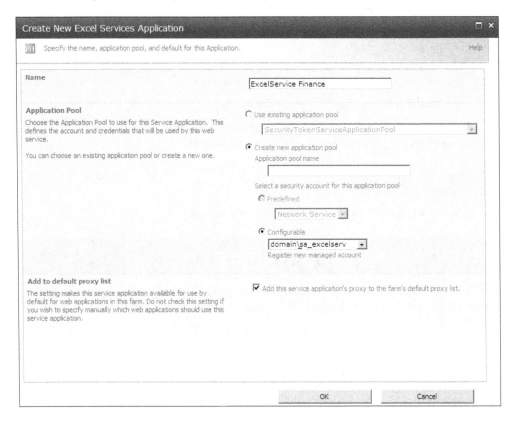

❑ **Name**: This is the name for the service application. Name the Service Application as **ExcelService Finance**.

❑ **Application Pool**: Create a new application pool here or use an existing one.

❑ **Configurable**: This is a domain security account for the application pool.

❑ Check the **Add to default proxy list** option. Refer to the *Creating a Custom Service Application Proxy group* recipe. For this recipe, check the box so that it will be tied to the default.

5. Ensure that there is a running Secure Store Service by checking that the service is started on the **Manage Service Applications** page. If it is not, follow the *Creating the Secure Store* recipe.

6. Set up the unattended service account in the Secure Store. Click on **Application Management** and then select **Manage service applications**.

7. Navigate to the **Secure Store Service** and click on it. It should appear as a hyperlink.

8. The screen that displays is where we create the **Target Application Settings**. Click **New** on the ribbon. You will be presented with the following screen:

9. Fill in the fields as follows:

❑ **Target Application ID**: CBExcelServices

❑ **Display Name: Cook Book Excel Services**

❑ **E-mail**: Use an e-mail address from your domain

❑ **Target Application Type**: Change to **Group** from **Individual** that is set by default

❑ **Target Application Page URL**: Select the **None** option

10. Click **Next**.

11. The next screen displays the fields that will be stored in the target application. Leave them as they are and click **Next**.

12. Finally, the administrator and members of the group must be input via the following screen:

Target Application Administrators

The list of users who have access to manage the Target Application settings. The farm administrator will have access by default.

Users who have Full Control or All Target Applications privileges can administer this Secure Store Target Application.

  ❑ **Target Application Administrators**: Enter the user who will have administrator access.

13. Click **OK**.

14. Now a user credential needs to be set up for this target application. Click **Set Credentials** on the ribbon with the **CBExcelServices** option checked. Refer to the following screenshot:

15. The next screen needs the credential users for Excel Services. Enter the following information:

  ❑ **Credential Owner**

  ❑ **Windows User Name**

  ❑ **Windows Password / Confirm Windows Password**

Click **OK**.

16. On the **Manage Service Applications** page, click to the right of the service application called **ExcelService Finance**. The ribbon at the top will light up. Note that the Service Application is the left-aligned object, whereas the Service Application Proxy is the indented object with the same name.

17. Click the **Manage** option on the ribbon. The following screenshot will appear for configuration:

Global Settings
Define load balancing, memory, and throttling thresholds. Set the unattended service account and data connection timeouts.

Trusted File Locations
Define places where spreadsheets can be loaded from.

Trusted Data Providers
Add or remove data providers that can be used when refreshing data connections.

Trusted Data Connection Libraries
Define a SharePoint Document Library where data connections can be loaded from.

User Defined Function Assemblies
Register managed code assemblies that can be used by spreadsheets.

18. Click **Global Settings**.

19. The Excel Service setting form will appear. At the bottom, there is a spot to fill in **Application ID** for the unattended service account. Use the account that was set up in step 6.

Application ID:

CBExcelServices

Valid Values: <=256 characters. Must exist in the registered Secure Store Service Application.

20. Click **OK**.

How it works...

The first important milestone in our recipe happens after Step 4. When we fill out this form and click the **Create** button, the Excel Services Application and associated service proxy are created and started. In SQL, a database is created and now the web front-end and the application server can communicate using web services (WCF). Refer to the *Managing a service* recipe for the explanation on the web service.

In Step 16, we needed an unattended service account for the ExcelService Finance Service Application. This account gives us the ability to access our back-end data that is utilized in our workbooks. This is set up in steps from 5 through 12.

I want to point out that in step 8, there is a **Target Application Type** setting; for this recipe, we choose **Individual**. We could have chosen **group**, which is the current recommendation. The advantage of doing this is that we can create a group in Active Directory and apply it to our unattended service account. Then, we only need to manage the users in that group instead of coming back to the Secure Store.

Group management is the preferred method, most of the time.

There's more...

Creation of the Excel Services Application can be achieved using scripts, through the use of PowerShell. Here are the associated PowerShell commands:

```
Get-SPExcelServiceApplication -identity <name of service app>
Set-SPExcelServiceApplication -identity <name of service app>
New-SPExcelServiceApplication -name <name>
```

More info

As seen in Step 8, there are a few more configuration options that can be set. The one that is important to be aware of is **Trusted File Locations**. By default, the root site is set. This is significant because it means that workbooks can be loaded from anywhere in the farm. This is a new behavior in SharePoint 2010.

See also

 ▶ *Managing a service*
 ▶ *Creating the Secure Store*

Setting up PerformancePoint Services

PerformancePoint Services give a user the ability to create KPIs, scorecards, and dashboards from data typically not contained within SharePoint. However, SharePoint list data can be used as a data source.

PerformancePoint exceeds expectations when it uses a SQL Server Analysis cube as its datasource. The reason for this is that now information can be leveraged in the dashboard and can be viewed multiple ways. Another common term for this is slicing and dicing the data. This ability comes from data set up in a cube. PerformancePoint does not set up a cube, but rather consumes the data and provides a mechanism to display and drill down into that data.

The second place PerformancePoint shines is in its ability to use several different technologies and provide a single viewing source for them. For example, a dashboard can be set up with several web part zones. One zone could be showing the scorecards of a process, the second zone could be showing a SQL Reporting Services report of that process. The third zone could show the Excel spreadsheets that are related to that process.

PerformancePoint Services is a single farm service. This means it cannot be shared across farms. In this recipe, we will show how to set up and configure a PerformancePoint Service.

Getting ready

You must have Farm Administrator privileges to Central Administration.

Ensure that there is a web application already set up. In most cases it will be called SharePoint – 80.

How to do it...

1. Open **Central Administration** and click **Application Management**.

2. The third section is **Service Applications**. Under it, click **Manage Service applications**.

3. On the ribbon, select **New | PerformancePoint Service Application**.

4. You will get the following screenshot. Fill in the required details.

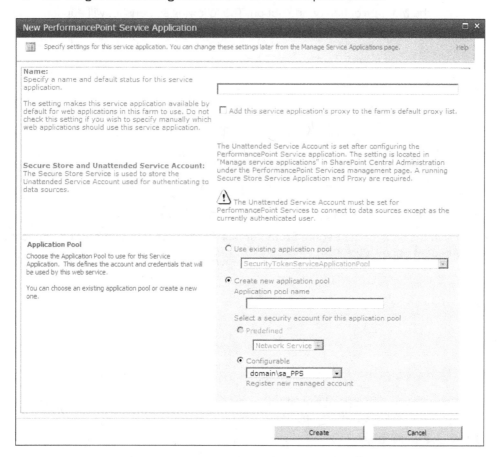

□ **Name**: This is the name for the service application. Name the Service Application as **PPS Finance**.

□ Check the **Add this service application's proxy...** option.

□ **Application Pool**: Create a new application pool here or use an existing one.

□ **Configurable**: This is a domain security account for the application pool.

5. Click on the **Create** button.

6. Ensure that there is a running Secure Store Service by checking that the service is started on the **Manage Service Applications** page. If it is not, follow the *Creating the Secure Store* recipe.

7. On the **Manage Service Applications** page, click to the right of the PerformancePoint service application called **PPS Finance**. The ribbon on the top will light up. Note that the Service Application is the left-aligned object, whereas the Service Application Proxy is the indented object with the same name.

8. Click the **Manage** option on the ribbon. The following screenshot will appear for configuration:

9. Click the **PerformancePoint Service Application Settings** option.

10. Fill in the data for the **Secure Store Service Application** and **Unattended Service Account** option. Click **OK**.

11. Open up your SharePoint website. This will be the site that is associated to the web application where PerformancePoint has been set up.

12. Click **Site Settings**.

13. Under **Site Collection Administration**, click the **Site Collection Features** option.

14. Click on the **Activate** button on **SharePoint Publishing Infrastructure**:

15. Navigate back to **Site Settings** (Step 11). Click **Manage site features** under **Site Actions**.
16. Click on the **Activate** button on **PerformancePoint Services Site Features**.

How it works...

This was a coordinated series of steps that activated many moving parts in our SharePoint installation. It is important to understand what was done under the covers.

The first important milestone in our recipe happens after Step 4. When we fill out this form and click **Create**, the PPS Application and associated service proxy are created and started. In SQL, a database is created and now the web front-end and the application server can communicate using web services (WCF) to the database. Refer to *Managing a Service* recipe for the explanation of the web service.

In Step 9, we needed an unattended service account for PPS Finance. This account gives us the ability to access our back-end data that will be shown in our dashboards and utilized in our KPIs and scorecards.

Finally in Steps 13 and 15, we activated the features necessary on our site to utilize PerformancePoint Services. The first feature was the publishing infrastructure. This is necessary as it provides publishing components that are necessary for the Business Intelligence Center.

The second feature was the PerformancePoint components that are utilized. These are the PerformancePoint content types, web parts, and a Business Intelligence Center site template found under **Enterprise**. Here is an example of the content types that are created:

There's more...

Creation of the PerformancePoint Application can be achieved with the help of scripts, through the use of PowerShell. Here are the associated PowerShell commands:

PowerShell: PerformancePoint Cmdlets

```
New-SPPerformancePointServiceApplication

Remove-SPPerformancePointServiceApplication

Get-SPPerformancePointServiceApplication

New-SPPerformancePointServiceApplicationProxy

Remove-SPPerformancePointServiceApplicationProxy
```

See also

- ▸ *Managing a service*
- ▸ *Creating the Secure Store*

Setting up Visio Services

Using Visio to visualize the data in SharePoint enables users at all levels to understand an organization's processes. These processes touch users such as customers, vendors, suppliers, and employees within the organization.

The data that is being used in Visio does not have to exist in SharePoint, and can be external. It gives organizations the ability to take complex processes and create a **storyboard** out of them, which is a pictorial representation of a process. When processes are converted to storyboards, they can be evaluated and improved in an agile fashion.

This equates to leaner, more efficient processes, which ultimately equates to better decision making, happier customers, and informed vendors and suppliers. The end result will be new and repeat business and cost savings.

With Visio Services, organizations can view Visio diagrams through Visio web parts. In addition, Visio web parts can interact with other web parts, giving users the flexibility to create items such as mashups.

This recipe goes through the steps to set up Visio Services.

Getting ready

You must have Farm Administrator privileges to Central Administration.

How to do it...

1. Open the **Central Administration** screen and click **Application Management**.
2. The third section is **Service Applications**. Under it, click **Manage Service Applications**.
3. On the ribbon, select **New | Visio Graphics Service Application**.
4. You will get the following screen. Fill in the necessary data.

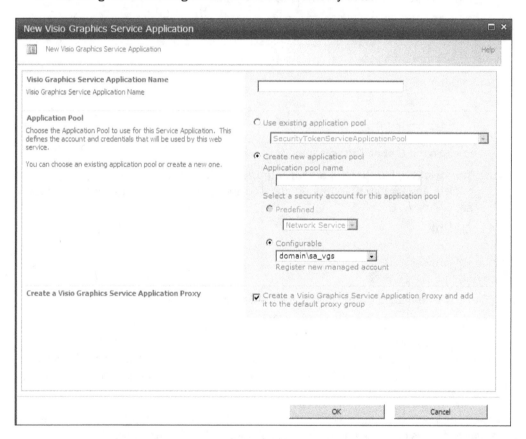

- ❑ **Visio Graphics Service Application Name**: Enter the name as **Visio Finance**.
- ❑ **Application Pool**: Create an application pool. Under **Configurable**, use an account that you have set up for the service.

      ❑   Check the **Visio Graphics Service Application Proxy** option to put it in the default proxy group.

Once you are done filling the required data, click **OK**.

5. Ensure that there is a running Secure Store Service by checking that the service is started on the **Manage Service Applications** page. If it is not, follow the *Creating the Secure Store* recipe.

6. Set up the unattended service account in the Secure Store. Refer to the steps from 5 through 12 of the *Setting up Excel Services* recipe.

7. On the **Manage Service Applications** page, click to the right of the Visio Graphics service application called **Visio Finance**. The ribbon at the top will light up. Note that the Service Application is the left-aligned object, whereas the Service Application Proxy is the indented object with the same name.

8. Click **Manage** on the ribbon. The following screenshot will appear for configuration:

> Global Settings
> Manage settings for performance, security, and refreshing data connections.
>
> Trusted Data Providers
> Add or remove data providers that can be used when refreshing data connections.

9. Click on the **Global Settings** option.

10. The Visio Graphics Service setting form will appear and at the bottom there is a spot to fill in **Application ID** for the unattended service account. Use the account that was set up in step 6.

11. Click **OK**.

How it works...

Visio Services is managed by the Visio Graphics Service application.

The first important milestone in our recipe happens after Step 4. When we fill in this form and click on the **Create** button, the Visio Services Application and associated service proxy are created and started. In SQL, a database is created and now the WFE and the application server can communicate using web services (WCF). Refer to the *Managing a Service* recipe for the explanation on the web service.

In step 10, we needed an unattended service account for Visio Finance. This account gives us the ability to access our back-end data that is utilized in the Visio web parts.

There's more...

Creation of the Visio Services Application can be achieved using scripts through the use of PowerShell. Here are the associated PowerShell commands.

PowerShell: Visio Cmdlets

```
New-SPVisioServiceApplication

Remove-SPVisioServiceApplication

Get-SPVisioServiceApplication

New-SPVisioServiceApplicationProxy

Remove-SPVisioServiceApplicationProxy
```

More info

Visio diagrams are viewed in the browser through Silverlight or as a PNG graphic. In order to utilize the Visio Web Access Web Part, enable Enterprise Site Collection Features on each site collection.

See also

▶ _Managing a Service_
▶ _Creating the Secure Store_

Setting up the Managed Metadata Service

The **Managed Metadata Service** (**MMS**) is critical to an efficient and functioning SharePoint 2010 site. It provides the means to define and share metadata within a farm, as well as across farms, from a central location. This also allows an organization to share content types across site collections and web applications.

The power of this becomes immediately apparent in organizations that take the time to structure their data. It is clear to see how an enterprise organization could benefit from this service. An example could be creating an FDA-approved drug in a large pharmaceutical company. This process is complex due to diverse geography, potential language barriers, federal regulations, stringent testing methods, and detailed accounting of every step of the process.

Upon identifying all of these elements, characteristics such as naming conventions, type of data, testing terminology, and internal terminology can be identified and made consistent. The Managed Metadata Service is the language of your business. This brings consistency and enforceability, resulting in palpable cost savings.

Take the example of Zach's Trucking Company. This national company has two server farms—one for project-related sites and the other dedicated to government business. A component such as Average Weight per Shipment is appropriate to both farms, but it would be inefficient and redundant to create this term in both farms. Also, the same individual may not create it in both farms, so there is the possibility that this term is referred to as *AWS* in one system and *Avg Wgt* in the other.

Enter the Managed Metadata service. Both farms would consume this service, which contains this one term in the term store.

One of the farms must be the source, the publisher of the MMS. This is where the management of the MMS takes place. The other farm is the consumer, a subscriber to the service.

In this recipe, we will be creating a Managed Metadata Service Application.

Getting ready

You must have Farm Administrator privileges to Central Administration.

How to do it...

1. Open Central Administration and click **Application Management**.
2. The third section is **Service Applications**. Under it, click **Manage Service Applications**.
3. On the ribbon, select **New | Manage Metadata Service**.
4. The following screen appears. Fill in the required information.

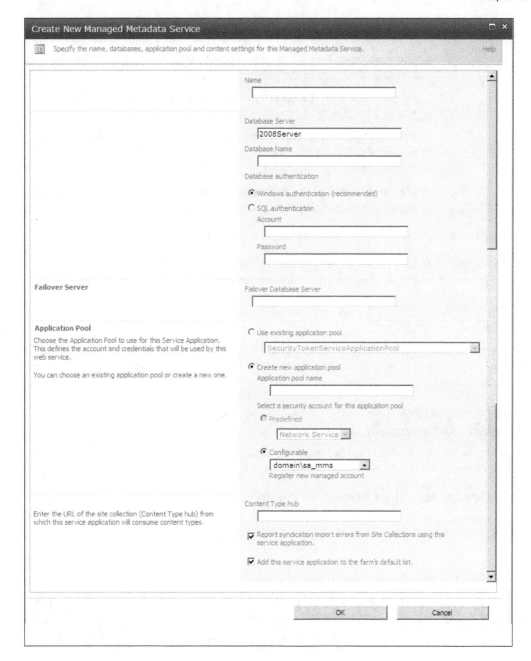

- **Name**: The name of the Managed Metadata Service.
- **Database Server**: The SQL Server where the MMS database is located.
- **Database authentication**: In most cases, use **Windows authentication**.

- ❑ **Failover Database Server**: This is the database server that has already been set up as a failover server. This does not set it up, it only references it.

- ❑ **Application Pool**: This is the account that contains the identity to reference the Managed Metadata Service web services.

- ❑ Enter the URL for the **Content Type hub**. Refer to the *Adding a Content Type Hub* recipe in *Chapter 8, Content Management,* for an explanation.

- ❑ Check the **Report syndication import errors...** option. This will report errors in the log of the site collections, that is, the exporting as well as the importing site.

- ❑ Check the **Add this to the farm's default list** option. Refer to the *Managing Service Applications Associations* recipe if you wish to change this.

5. Once you fill in the required information, click **OK**.

The Managed Metadata Service is now added to the **Service Applications** list and needs to be configured through the **Manage** option on the ribbon.

How it works...

The Managed Metadata Service process creates a database whose name is given by the user in Step 4. A connection is created to the MMS web services through the default service application proxy.

There's more...

Creating the Managed Metadata Services Application can be done with scripts through the use of PowerShell. Here are the associated PowerShell commands.

PowerShell: Managed Metadata Cmdlets

```
New-SPMetadataServiceApplication -ApplicationPool
"<ApplicationPoolName>" -Name "<ServiceName>" -DatabaseName
"<DatabaseName>" -DatabaseServer "<DatabaseServerName>" -HubUri
"<HubURI>"
```

Establishing a trust relationship between two farms

To be able to subscribe to another farm's content, there has to be a trust relationship set up between the two farms. This gives the two server farms, the ability to communicate. This is accomplished through certificates that uniquely identify the farms.

In this recipe you will see how to set this up.

Getting ready

Because we are showing this with PowerShell, you must be a member of the `SharePoint_Shell_Access` database role on the configuration database of both the publishing farm and consuming farm. You also must be a member of the `WSS_ADMIN_WPG` local group on the chosen servers.

Finally, the two servers you will be using (one on the Publishing Farm and one on the Consuming Farm) must be selected ahead of time and the same two servers must be used throughout the process. The suggested servers to use are the ones hosting Central Administration.

How to do it...

Export the certificates: Publishing Farm

1. On the chosen publishing farm server, select **Start | All Programs | Microsoft SharePoint 2010 Products | SharePoint 2010 Management Shell**.

2. In the PowerShell command prompt, type in the following two commands:

```
$rootCert = (Get-SPCertificateAuthority).RootCertificate

$rootCert.Export("Cert")|Set-Content C:\pubfarm.cer -Encoding byte
```

Export the certificates: Consuming Farm

3. On the consuming farm server, select **Start | All Programs | Microsoft SharePoint 2010 Products | SharePoint 2010 Management Shell**.

4. In the PowerShell command prompt, type in the following four commands:

```
$rootCert = (Get-SPCertificateAuthority).RootCertificate

$rootCert.Export("Cert")|Set-Content C:\consumingfarm.cer -Encoding byte

$stsCert=(Get-SPSecurityTokenServiceConfig) LocalLoginProvider.SigningCertificate

$stsCert.Export("Cert")|Set-Content c:\consumingfarmsts.cer -Encoding byte
```

Import the certificates: Publishing Farm

5. Copy the `consumingfar.cer` and the `consumingfarmsts.cer` file from the consuming farm and put them in the `C:\temp` folder on the chosen server in the publishing farm.

6. In the PowerShell command prompt, type in the following four commands:

    ```
    $trustCert=GetPfxCertificate c:\temp\consumingfarm.cer

    New-SPTrustedRootAuthority ConsumingFarm –Certificate $trustCert

    $stsCert=GetPFXCertificate c:\temp\consumingfarmsts.cer

    New-SPTrustedServiceTokenIssuer ConsumingFarm -Certificate
    $stsCert
    ```

Import the certificates: Consuming Farm

7. Copy the `pubfarm.cer` file from the publishing farm and put it in the `C:\temp` folder on the consuming farm.

8. In the PowerShell command prompt, type in the following two commands:

    ```
    $trustCert=GetPfxCertificate c:\temp\pubfarm.cer

    New-SPTrustedRootAuthority PublishingFarm –Certificate $trustCert
    ```

How it works...

Step 2 under *How to do it...* section comprises of two parts—setting the `$rooCert` variable to `RootCertificate` and then exporting that certificate to a physical file, `pubfarm.cer`.

Step 4 does the same thing except the fact that this is an extra step to provide the publishing farm with a **Security Token Service** (**STS**) certificate.

In steps 6 and 8, there are two italicized parameters—`ConsumingFarm` and `PublishingFarm`. These are unique names created by us as administrators. The names represent the purpose of the farm. It is recommended to give them more meaningful names so that their purpose is clear.

Both the publishing and consuming farms must exchange certificates. In addition, the consuming farm must export a security token service certificate, which the publishing farm imports.

Most of the service applications utilize web services to access the SharePoint databases. Web services do this on behalf of an authenticated client. In SharePoint 2010, it is the STS that authenticate clients. The clients in this chapter are service applications who provide credentials to the STS. Once authenticated, the STS issues a security token to the service application, which is their "passport" to obtain the information they are requesting.

There's more...

While exporting must be done with PowerShell, there is a user interface in Central Administration for importing certificates.

1. Navigate to Central Administration and click **Security**.
2. Under the **General Security** section, click **Manage trust**.

The ribbon will light up after clicking on the name of the farm. Now you can click **New** to establish a trust relationship, or you can click **Edit** to modify the Token issuer description or the certificates that are used.

Finally, there is a **Delete** option to allow you to remove a trust relationship.

Publishing a SharePoint service

One of the key advantages of service applications is their ability to be consumed on an a la carte level. Use the service only as you need it. Extending this paradigm further, service applications are similar to services in a cloud. Use what you need, no matter what farm you are using.

This gives organizations the ability to pool their resources effectively. An example of a resource that could be shared is content types. Many organizations are ISO certified and as such they are required to collect particular information with regards to their documents. A content type can be set up to which custom fields are assigned. For example, we could create a field called **Safety Training Date** and assign that to the content type.

As the SharePoint installation grows, more web applications and site collections are created. The organization does not want to recreate the content type that contains the field safety training date in each farm. By publishing the metadata service, other farms can consume this service and no redundancy is created. Further, maintenance of the content type is from a central location providing consistency and timeliness. The organization can adapt easily to change.

In order to use another service application, it must be made available. This is referred to as publishing the service.

Getting ready

You must have local administrative permissions to the SharePoint 2010 web front-end (WFE) and have Farm Administrator privileges to Central Administration.

How to do it...

1. Open the **Central Administration** screen and click **Application Management**.

2. The third section is **Service Applications**. Under it click **Manage Service Applications**.

3. Navigate to the service you will be publishing. Click to the right of the service name and check to see that the ribbon has lit up. The chosen service should look like the following screenshot:

4. Click **Publish** on the ribbon. The following form appears:

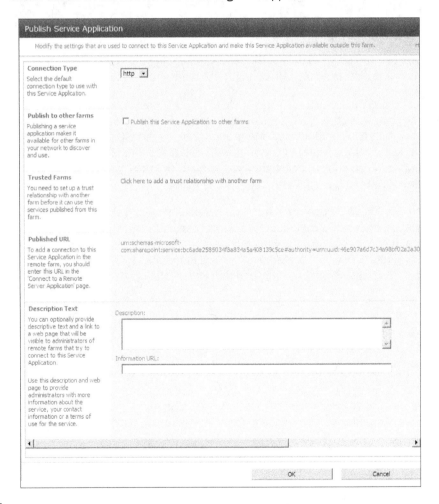

Fill in the required information.

- ❏ **Connection Type**: Use **http** from the available drop-down list.
- ❏ **Publish to other Farms**: Check this box.
- ❏ **Trusted Farms**: Use this link to create a new trust relationship. This process is detailed in the recipe called *Establishing a trust relationship between two farms*.
- ❏ **Published URL**: This URL will be used when we consume another farm's service. Copy this to Notepad for reference.
- ❏ **Description Text**: This is an informational description and URL where you provide information about the service. Provide a description that gives supporting information as to why this is being done.
- ❏ **Information URL**: Provide the link to the web page that has been set up previously. Include a description text that gives an explanation about the trust being set up.

Once you have filled in the required information, click **OK**.

How it works...

The key component in publishing a service is the Published URL. This is created when publishing a service. It is the reference back to the service being published.

The URL will be provided to the consuming farm. This should be copied to a separate location so that the administrators know where to reference it.

There's more...

Publishing a Service Application can be done with the help of scripts, through the use of PowerShell. Here is the associated Powershell command:

PowerShell: Publishing Service Cmdlet

```
Publish-SPServiceApplication -Identity <ServiceApplicationGUID>
```

More info

Only the following service applications can be published between SharePoint farms:

- ▸ Business Data Connectivity
- ▸ Managed Metadata
- ▸ People
- ▸ Search
- ▸ Secure Store
- ▸ Web Analytics

See also

- ▸ *Establishing a trust relationship between two farms*
- ▸ *Consuming another farm's service*

Consuming another Farm's Service

Service applications can consume another service application. The advantage of this capability is leveraging resources that are defined and managed from a central location and distributed throughout the farm and/or farms.

Using the managed metadata service example from publishing, redundancy is reduced through reuse. The field created in one web application/site collection can be consumed in a completely separate web application/site collection. Maintenance of the content type is from a central location providing consistency and timeliness. As business and needs change, the organization can adapt quickly.

In this recipe, we will show how to consume another service application.

Getting ready

You must have local administrative permissions to the SharePoint 2010 web front-end (WFE) and have Farm Administrator privileges to Central Administration.

If you are consuming a service from another farm, a trust must be set up between farms. Refer to the *Establishing a trust relationship between farms* recipe on how to perform this action.

How to do it...

1. Open the Central Administration screen and click **Application Management**.
2. The third section is **Service Applications**. Under it, click **Manage Service Application**.
3. Navigate the listing until your mouse is over the **Manage Metadata Service** option. The bar should be blue.
4. The second ribbon component is **Connect**. Click the down arrow and seek the listing call **Managed Metadata Service Connection**. Choose this by clicking on it. The following screenshot will appear:

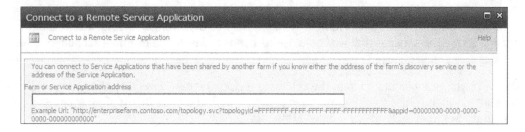

5. Copy the published URL that was saved in step 4 of *Publishing a SharePoint Service* recipe. After clicking **OK**, the following screenshot will appear:

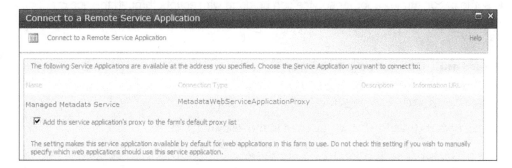

6. Click on the **Managed Metadata Service** link. Now the **OK** option will be enabled. After clicking **OK**, the following screenshot will appear:

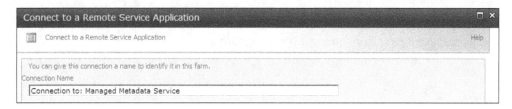

7. You may rename the connection. Leave this value to default and click **OK**.

The service is now connected.

How it works...

The Application Discovery and Load Balancer Service Application are the means by which farms know which service application are available to be consumed. This service is also referred to as the Topology Service.

When we published the service application, a URL was automatically created that we used as the input to step 4. This URL is what the Topology Service discovers. In step 5, the topology service shows the services that we could use as connections. In the example explained here, there is only one to choose.

Once everything is completed from the consume recipe, the new service application being consumed will appear with the name given in step 7 (referred to as **Connect to: Managed Metadata Service**) under the Managed Metadata Service.

There's more...

The setup of consuming another service can be done with scripts through the use of PowerShell. Here are the two associated PowerShell commands that must be run in the order shown:

PowerShell: Consuming Cmdlets

```
Receive-SPSharedServiceApplicationInfo -FarmUrl
<PublishingFarmTopologyURL>
```

This step obtains the URL that will be used in the following step.

```
SP-ServiceApplicationProxy -Name"<ServiceApplicationProxyName>" -Url
"<PublishingFarmTopologyURL>"
```

See also

- ▸ *Publishing a SharePoint service*
- ▸ *Establishing a trust relationship between farms*

3
Farm Governance

In this chapter, we will cover:

- ▸ Administering SharePoint Designer
- ▸ Configuring a Managed account
- ▸ Creating a new policy for web application
- ▸ Configuring Resource Throttling (large lists)
- ▸ Installing a feature and activating it
- ▸ Restricting web parts access in the farm
- ▸ Learning timer job management (including server affinity)
- ▸ Running a timer job on demand
- ▸ Configuring Sandbox functionality

Introduction

Governance is a large topic on its own. There are books dedicated solely to this topic. What is being covered in relation to governance are ten items that, when used, makes your life as administrator a bit easier.

An administrator's job is akin to being the Marines. They are the first ones to be called when there is an issue with SharePoint. Nothing gets done without their knowledge. Typically, the administrator has to decide who to bring in when an issue needs to be addressed. Additionally, administrators deal with management, end users, developers, and the power users.

The recipes in this chapter teach and expose useful and common functionality found in SharePoint 2010. The intent of the recipes is to create a SharePoint Farm environment that is efficient and monitored. For example, large lists have always been an issue in SharePoint in the past, with little or no support to address it out of the box. This is directly related to the performance of your SharePoint installation. This chapter has a recipe on a new functionality, throttling large lists.

As we have seen in other chapters, PowerShell is a critical tool for the SharePoint Administrator. While the recipes may only show how to use the commands at a granular level, they may be combined to create powerful administrator scripts.

As a result, many of the tasks that are performed today can be automated and collected at a macro level. After reading this chapter, think about how these techniques can be combined.

Administering SharePoint Designer

SharePoint Designer 2010 is a powerful tool that helps create rapid solutions using SharePoint. As the tool is free, any user can download and access its functionality. By connecting to a SharePoint site, users can freely make significant changes to the site. This includes the look and feel of the site, workflow, and connecting to external sources.

The issue with this amount of power is the havoc that can be done by creating customizations that inadvertently tax the SharePoint Server(s). The end result may be a degradation of the responsiveness of the SharePoint farm, adversely affecting the performance of the site.

Let's look at the preceding paragraph in terms of a real workflow as an example. Workflows are very popular and can be done out of the box with SharePoint Designer. Zach's trucking company hauls product all over the country. They get their work responding to a Request for Quotation. They can get up to ten RFQs per day.

The requirement is that when an RFQ document gets uploaded, several tasks are created in a separate list for multiple people. Using the task list, they can determine when the document is ready to be sent out.

The workflow can be created in SharePoint Designer (SPD) out of the box. If the person using SharePoint Designer is not well-versed in creating workflows, it is possible that he/she might create long running tasks and infinite loops. Over time, the farm performance will degrade. This is because at the heart of SharePoint, every call made goes back to the SQL database. An infinite loop could cause a list to become quite large.

A different issue has to do with usability and standards. As users with proper permissions can modify look and feel of individual sites, they can deviate from corporate standards. Multiply this capability with the number of users in your organization, and you will realize there is a very real issue with governance of sites in general.

SharePoint 2010 has a solution for these problems that can either limit a user's capability in their site or take it away completely. This recipe shows you how and where to do this within SharePoint.

Getting ready

You must have farm level administrative permissions to the Central Administration site.

How to do it...

1. Open up the SharePoint 2010 Central Administration website.

2. Click **Application Management**. Under the **Web Applications** section, click **Manage Web Applications**.

3. The available web applications will be listed. Click to the right of the web application you wish to manage. The entire line will turn blue and the ribbon will light up. If you have installed SharePoint into the default instance, it may look like the following screenshot:

| SharePoint - 80 | http://2008server/ | 80 |

4. On the ribbon, there is a button called **General Settings**. Click on that button and select the **SharePoint Designer** option from the drop-down list that appears.

5. The following screenshot appears:

Fill in the required information:

❏ **Allow SharePoint Designer to be used in this Web Application**: Unchecking this box will disable SPD for the entire web application.

❏ **Allow Site Collection Administrators to Detach Pages from the Site Template**: Once this option is unchecked, Site Administrators will not be able to detach pages and modify them via SPD.

❏ **Allow Site Collection Administrators to Customize Master Pages and Layout Pages**: If it is unchecked, Site Administrators will not be able to customize pages via SPD.

❏ **Allow Site Collection Administrators to see the URL Structure of their Web Site**: If unchecked, it will not allow Site Collection Administrators to manage the URL structure via SPD.

How it works...

SharePoint Designer is a client application that is installed on the user's desktop. This recipe shows how to disable SPD from working at a web application level.

There's more...

The Site Collection Administrator can also modify the way SharePoint Designer works. To accomplish this:

1. Open up the **Site Collection** screen and click **Site Settings**.

2. In the section under **Site Collection Administration**, there is an entry call **SharePoint Designer Settings**; select that.

3. The following form appears:

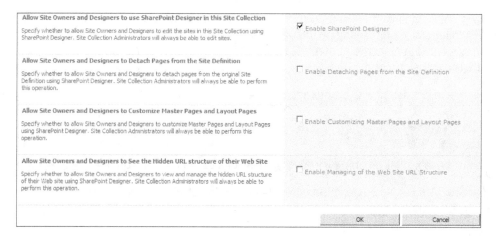

The sections are self-explanatory.

If the Farm Administrator limits SPD access at the Central Administration level (as shown earlier in the recipe), the changes are reflected in red color on the form, with a message as seen in the following screenshot:

Configuring a Managed account

A Managed account in SharePoint is an account that is completely managed by Active Directory.

Service accounts are a prime example. These accounts are typically domain-level accounts that are managed in Active Directory (AD). Being an active directory account means it is subject to the policies implemented across the organization. For example, a user may have to change their password every six months. The policy may dictate that the password meet certain criteria such as containing upper case and lower case characters.

The problem with this scenario in SharePoint terms occurs when the password needs to be changed. The service stops working when the password expires. If the account is the identity for multiple services, they stop working too, which potentially brings a working SharePoint installation to a stop.

In many organizations, there is a division of responsibilities that can prohibit the SharePoint Farm Administrator from changing the password of an AD account. The Managed account resolves this issue. SharePoint manages this account and, through central administration, you can register these accounts.

In this recipe, we see how to create and manage an account.

Getting ready

You must have farm-level administrative permissions to the Central Administration site.

The account that you are configuring must be set up in Active Directory. It must be an existing AD account.

How to do it...

1. Open up the SharePoint 2010 Central Administration website.
2. Click **Security**.
3. Under the section titled **General Security**, select the **Configure managed accounts** option.
4. Click **Register Managed Account**. The following form appears:

Account Registration

Service accounts are used by various farm components to operate. The account password can be set to automatically change on a schedule and before any scheduled Active Directory enforced password change event.

Enter the service account credentials.

Service account credentials
User name

Password

Automatic Password Change

Automatic password change enables SharePoint to automatically generate new strong passwords on a schedule you set. Select the Enable automatic password change checkbox to allow SharePoint to manage the password for the selected account.

If an account policy based expiry date is detected for the account, and the expiry will occur before the scheduled date and time, the password will be changed on a configured number of days before the expiry date at the regularly scheduled time.

Choose to enable e-mail notifications in order to have the system generate warning notifications about upcoming password change events.

Specify a time and schedule for the system to automatically change the password.

☐ Enable automatic password change
If password expiry policy is detected, change password

[2] days before expiry policy is enforced

☐ Start notifying by e-mail

[5] days before password change

○ Weekly

● Monthly

Fill in the required information:

- ❑ **User name**: Supply the AD account. It does not have to be prefaced with domain.
- ❑ **Password**: This must match the account password in AD.
- ❑ **Enable automatic password change**: Checking this will allow you to set the time and notifications by e-mail.

When finished filling the required data, click **OK**. The account is now added.

How it works...

When the account is added as shown in the recipe, its credentials are now managed and stored within SharePoint. SharePoint 2010 can leverage the AD policies to automatically reset passwords.

Once the account is in SharePoint, it is encrypted using the farm encryption key that was specified when the farm was created based on the passphrase. A key benefit of using managed accounts is the ability conferred upon the Farm Administrator to join machines to the farm without specifying the credentials.

There's more...

PowerShell can be used to do anything you can do through the Central Administration user interface.

Powershell: Get a listing of managed accounts

```
Get-SPManagedAccount
```

Powershell: Create a new account

```
New-SPManagedAccount
```

Powershell: Set

```
Set-SPManagedAccount -identity
```

Powershell: Delete a managed account

```
Remove-SPManagedAccount
```

More info

You cannot use the Central Administration UI to assign local accounts to be managed accounts. This is achievable, but only through PowerShell.

Creating a new policy for a web application

There are times when it is critical for the Farm Administrator to designate security policies for a web application. An administrator can do this from Central Administration and it overrides security implemented at the site collection and at sub-site level.

The following are some useful scenarios where this may be implemented:

▶ Enterprise organizations need to designate at least one person as the Site Administrator. Once assigned, they are now the administrator of the web application. This is not to be confused with the Farm Administrator or a Site Collection Administration.

▶ When bringing sites online, it is advantageous to set up security to deny access to all users. Allow access to only those users who are your beta users. After the site is live, you can remove these restrictions.

In this recipe, we will show how to create a new policy and then add users to it.

Getting ready

You must have farm-level administrative permissions to the Central Administration site. There must be a web application set up.

How to do it...

1. Open up the SharePoint 2010 Central Administration website.

2. Click **Application Management**.

3. Under the first section named **Web Applications**, click **Manage web applications**.

4. Click the web application and see the ribbon light up. The rightmost button is **Permission Policy**; click on it. Refer to the next screenshot:

5. A pop-up form appears, click **Add Permission Policy Level**.

6. The following screen appears:

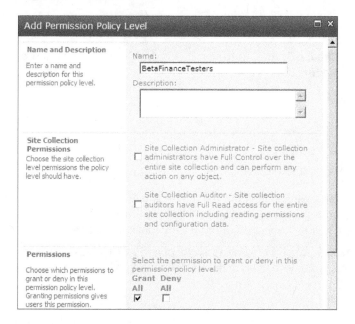

The list is comprised of five components:

- ❑ **Name**: Create a name for the permission level with a description.

- ❑ **Site Collection Permissions**: Selecting the **Administrator** option automatically grants read and write access to everything. Selecting **Auditor** for the site collection gives read access to everything.

- ❑ **List Permissions**: Granular control to deny or grant rights over objects at a list level.

- ❑ **Site Permissions**: Granular control to deny or grant rights over objects at a site level.

- ❑ **Personal Permissions**: Gives the users in this policy control over personal views and web parts.

For the purposes of this recipe, do not select site collection administration or auditor. Check **Grant All**. Click **Save**.

BetaFinanceTesters now appears in the listing of permissions policy.
Click **OK**.

7. On the web application page, click **User Policy** on the ribbon.

8. A screen is displayed, showing users who have a policy for the web application. Click the **Add Users** link.

9. A wizard pop-up is presented. Choose the **All zones** option from the drop-down list. Click **Next**.

10. On the ensuing form:

- ❑ Select a user (or group).

- ❑ Under **Choose Permissions**, check **BetaFinanceTesters**.

- ❑ **Choose System Settings**. Do not check the box **Account operates as System** box.

11. Click **Finish**.

How it works...

This recipe is broken into two parts:

- ▶ **Setting the permissions policy**: In steps 4 to 8, we defined a custom policy that was consequently saved in SharePoint. This policy defines the rights of the users that will belong to it. It is associated with the web application chosen.

  In our recipe, we showed how to add a policy. By clicking on an existing policy, it can be edited. There is also an option to delete the policy.

▸ **Designating users to that policy**: In steps 9 to 11, we are selecting users or group accounts and then assigning the custom permission level to them.

Users can also be deleted or their permissions edited via step 9.

There's more...

You cannot utilize SharePoint groups with Policy for web applications. However, you can use groups from Active Directory.

Configuring Resource Throttling (large lists)

At the very heart of SharePoint are lists. Just about everything in SharePoint is a list. It can be stated that SharePoint content is list driven.

One of the shortcomings of the previous version of SharePoint was that performance began to degrade if a list had more than 2000 items. This doesn't mean if a list had 2001 items, the performance degradation was noticeable. A SharePoint list could have millions of records. Let's break down exactly what happens when a user requests information from a list.

A user clicks on a link to see the items in a list. It invokes a query back to SQL to pull those items and present them. The query looks at how many columns are on that list and does a "select all" operation. The more columns in a list, the more data that is returned, and the longer it takes to select all of that data because it is number of rows multiplied by number of columns.

Resource throttling is a set of configuration items built into the software to address the issue of performance of large lists and resource contention. The goal is to prevent servers from running out of resources. Setting these parameters will offer better fidelity to your SharePoint installation.

In this recipe we will cover the different parameters and how to configure them.

Getting ready

You must have farm-level administrative permissions to the Central Administration site.

How to do it...

1. Open up the SharePoint 2010 Central Administration website.
2. Click **Application Management**.
3. Under the **Web Applications** section, click **Manage web applications**.
4. Select a web application (the ribbon will light up).

5. Click the **General Settings** dropdown on the ribbon:

6. Click the **Resource Throttling** option from the drop-down list. The resulting form has the following components to be configured:

    ❑   **List View Threshold**: Defaults to **5000**.

    ❑   **Object Model Override** – Yes/No radio buttons. The default value is **Yes**.

    ❑   **List View Threshold for Auditors and Administrators**: Defaults to **20000**.

    ❑   **List View Lookup threshold**: Defaults to **6**.

    ❑   **Daily Time Window for Large Queries**: Check this option which, when enabled, allows setting of a start time and a maximum duration.

    ❑   **List Unique Permissions Threshold**: Defaults to **50000**.

    ❑   **Backward-Compatible Event Handlers**: On/Off radio buttons. Defaults to **Off**.

    ❑   **HTTP Request Monitoring and Throttling**: On/Off radio buttons. Defaults to **On**.

    ❑   **Change Log**: Defaults to **60** days after which log entries are deleted. Can be set to **Never**.

    After making changes to any component(s), click **OK**.

How it works...

Resource throttling is performed at the web application level. The configuration applies to all site collections and sites under the web application. Throttling can be completely disabled in Central Administration for a web application, as seen in the parameter **HTTP Request Monitoring and Throttling**.

By default, resource throttling checking is on, which enables a timer job that runs every five seconds. This job checks the state of server resources against the performance counters. If that check comes back with a failure three times in a row, a throttling state will be enabled. The server will stay in this state until a successful check is performed.

While in a throttled state, users may see a 503 Server is busy screen. Users will need to refresh their screen to see if their request has completed.

The resources that are checked by default are Server CPU, Memory, Request in Queue, and Request Wait Time.

The **List View Threshold** is the number of items that can be returned to a user. By default, this is 5000 items.

The **List View threshold for Auditors and Administrators** is the number of items that can be returned to an administrator or power user. The default is 20000 items.

List View Loopup Threshold is the maximum amount of fields with the type called Lookup in a list. Lookups are database intensive. The default is 8.

List Unique Permissions Threshold is when inheritance is broken on a list and granular permissions are involved. Item-level permissions have potentially severe consequences on database performance and must be considered and planned carefully.

There's more...

PowerShell can be used to view, set, and enable/disable resource throttling.

PowerShell: View list of Performance Counters

```
Get-SPWebApplicationHttpThrottlingMonitor-identity <identity>
```

PowerShell: Set Performance Counters

```
Set-SPWebApplicationHttpThrottlingMonitor-identity <identity> -Category
<category> -Counter <counter> -Instance <instance> -MaxThreshold
<maxthreshold> -MinThreshold <minthreshold>
```

PowerShell: Disable Resource Throttling

```
Disable- SPWebApplicationHttpThrottlingMonitor-identity <identity>
```

PowerShell: Enable Resource Throttling

```
Enable- SPWebApplicationHttpThrottlingMonitor-identity <identity>
```

More info

Server CPU, Memory, Request in Queue, and Request Wait Time are monitored by default. A new performance counter has to be added via the object model. The counters that are used can be obtained via the Performance Monitor application on the server.

Here is an example of how to configure the Processor Time:

```
$uri = new-object System.Uri(http://"yourwebsite")
```

```
$webApp =
[Microsoft.SharePoint.Administration.SPWebApplication]::Lookup($uri)

$httpthrottlesettings = $webApp.HttpThrottleSettings

$httpthrottlesettings.AddPerformanceMonitor("Processor",
"% Processor Time", "_Total", 70,0)

$httpthrottlesettings.Update()
```

See also

 ▸ *Enabling HTTP Request Monitoring and Throttling*

Installing a feature and activating it

One of the tasks that inevitably fall upon a SharePoint Administrator is the process of installing features and solutions. Features are solutions typically written by developers. They perform a business function such as workflow or a web part.

With the advent of the SharePoint 2010 Sandbox, Site Collection Administrators can upload and maintain features. However, there are many situations in which a Farm Administrator needs to install a farm-wide feature.

Deploying a feature can be done through Visual Studio, but when implementing on production servers, this is not the way to install a feature. A feature in production should be installed by an administrator and this implies the use of PowerShell.

This recipe shows how to install a farm-wide feature and activate it.

Getting ready

You must have farm-level administrative permissions to the Central Administration site.

Feature must be deployed to the `14\template\features` folder.

How to do it...

1. Click on the **Start** button on the web front-end.
2. Under **All Programs**, navigate to the folder named `Microsoft SharePoint 2010 Products`.
3. Right-click on **SharePoint 2010 Management Shell** and click select **Run as Administrator**. The PowerShell console will appear.

4. Install the feature by typing the following into the console window:

   `Install-SPFeature -path "helloworld"`

   Press the *Enter* key.

5. Activate the feature by typing in the following command:

   `Enable-SPFeature -identity "helloworld" -URL http://sharepoint2010`

   Press the *Enter* key.

How it works...

The feature is installed on a web front-end server in the `\14\template\features\<features path>` folder. If the file is not there when doing the install, an error message will be displayed.

Features are best wrapped in a solution file. Solution files can be installed across a farm, which is efficient when dealing with a multi-server topology. It also can be installed to the Sandbox. In the recipe that was just presented, the feature was already deployed.

The following is how to install and deploy a solution file called `helloworld.wsp`:

1. Install the solution by typing the following command in the console window:

   `Add-SPSolution c:\temp\helloworld.wsp`

   Press *Enter*.

2. Deploy the solution by typing in:

   `Install-SPSolution -Identity helloworld.wsp -WebApplication`
   `http://sharepoint2010 -GACDeployment`

   Press the *Enter* key.

   Features that can be scoped at the following levels are seen in the next screenshot:

Farm	Activates a Feature for an entire server farm.
Site	Activates a Feature for all web sites in a site collection.
Web	Activates a Feature for a specific web site.
WebApplication	Activates a Feature for all web sites in a web application.

A solution file, `.wsp`, is a cab file that contains the following components:

- `Manifest.xml`: This file defines the features (there can be more than one), site definitions, resource files, web part files, and assemblies.
- `Feature.xml`: This file defines the location of the assemblies and defines the scope of the feature(s), and any dependencies.

- Elements.xml: This file contains information about the components being installed.
- The Assembly (DLL) being installed.

There's more...

To see all the installed features on your organizations' farm, use the PowerShell command, Get-SPFeature, with no scope.

Restricting web part access in the farm

Web parts are the components of an organization's site that provide modularity and flexibility. Web parts are ASP.NET server-side modules that are available to be put into a page via a web part zone. The modules perform all different kinds of functions based on an organization's needs.

SharePoint 2010 Enterprise comes with 60+ web parts. In addition, an organization can create their own web parts based on business requirements.

There are two considerations to think about with regards to governance of web parts in the context of this recipe.

- ▶ What a web part can be allowed to do
- ▶ What web parts are available to be put onto a page

Getting ready

You must have farm-level administrative permissions to the Central Administration site.

How to do it...

1. Open up SharePoint 2010 Central Administration website.
2. Click **Application Management**. Under the section **Web Applications**, click **Manage Web Applications**.
3. The available web applications will be listed. Click to the right of the web application you wish to manage. The entire line will turn blue and the ribbon will light up.
4. On the ribbon, there is a button called **Web Part Security**; click that. The following screenshot appears:

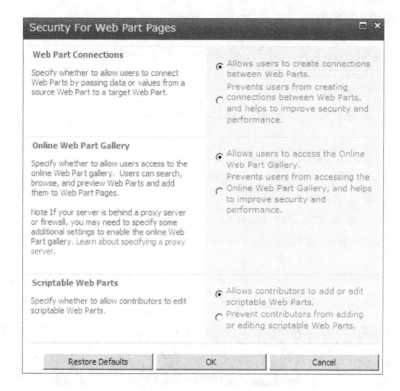

- **Web Part Connections**: The strength of web part connections is that information from one web part can be passed to another web part.

- **Online Web Part Gallery**: This is a web part gallery that is either available from Microsoft or one that has been created.

- **Scriptable Web Parts**: This will either allow or prevent contributors from adding scripts in a web part. An example of this is JavaScript in a Content Editor web part. Retain the default value.

Click **OK**.

How it works...

This recipe shows web part security at a web application level. Everything shown applies to all site collections under the web application. It works as a blanket policy. It is not web part security at a granular level.

There's more...

There are times when an organization needs to expose certain web parts to targeted users. Another way of saying this is managing which web parts appear in the Web Part Gallery based on a user's role.

The best way to do this is at a site collection level. You must be a Site Collection Administrator to do this.

1. Create the necessary SharePoint groups and add the appropriate users. Creating a matrix of groups and web parts will facilitate the actual assigning of permissions.

2. Select **Site Actions | Site Settings**.

3. Under the section named **Galleries**, select **Web Parts**.

4. Choose the web part that you wish to change permissions on by clicking the edit icon.

5. The form that appears has a ribbon with a button called **Manage Permissions**.

6. Adjust the permissions to represent the organization's needs.

Learning timer job management (including server affinity)

Timer job management is important when administering and monitoring the health of an organization's SharePoint installation. A timer job is a process that runs and performs some type of action. Timer jobs run in the farm on a specific server, which can be designated.

This recipe will show where and how to manage the timer jobs, including how to assign a server to timer jobs.

Getting ready

You must have farm-level administrative permissions to the Central Administration site.

How to do it...

1. Open up the SharePoint 2010 Central Administration website.

2. Click **Monitoring**. Under the second section named **Timer Jobs**, select the **Check Job Status** option.

3. The following information is displayed:

   - Timer jobs
   - The servers on which they are running

- ❑ The associated web application
- ❑ The status of each job
- ❑ The time when each job was finished or their scheduled start time

On the left-hand side of the screen are the categories for filtering the display of timer jobs, as shown in the following screenshot:

Timer Links

Timer Job Status

Scheduled Jobs

Running Jobs

Job History

Job Definitions

4. Let's now see how to edit a timer job.

   Click on the timer job called **Scheduled Approval**. The following form is displayed that enables the administrator to change the schedule, run the job now, or disable the job.

Job Title	Scheduled Approval
Job Description	The Approval Job is used to approve pages on a schedule.
Job Properties This section lists the properties for this job.	Web application: SharePoint - 80 Last run time: 5/14/2010 1:19 PM
Recurring Schedule Use this section to modify the schedule specifying when the timer job will run. Daily, weekly, and monthly schedules also include a window of execution. The timer service will pick a random time within this interval to begin executing the job on each applicable server. This feature is appropriate for high-load jobs which run on multiple servers on the farm. Running this type of job on all the servers simultaneously might place an unreasonable load on the farm. To specify an exact starting time, set the beginning and ending times of the interval to the same value.	This timer job is scheduled to run: ⊙ Minutes Every 1 minute(s) ○ Hourly ○ Daily ○ Weekly ○ Monthly

Run Now	Disable	OK	Cancel

5. The next task is to change the server where timer jobs run.

6. Click **Application Management**. Under the section called **Databases**, click **Manage content databases**.

7. Choose the **Web Application** option in the upper left corner.

8. The associated content database(s) are shown in the resulting listing. Click the content database link.

9. The form that gets displayed contains a myriad of database information related to the content database. At the bottom of the form is a section called **Preferred Server for Timer Jobs**.

The dropdown lists the available SharePoint Servers on which the timer jobs can be run. Select a server and click **OK**.

How it works...

Timer jobs are processes that are scheduled based on the Gregorian calendar. They run via the SharePoint Timer Service, known as OWSTIMER.EXE.

The jobs are stored in the SharePoint 2010 Content DB, in a table called `ScheduledWorkItems`.

There's more...

PowerShell is available to manage the timer jobs. We can have scripts that add business value and assist in managing timer jobs at a macro level, as opposed to managing timer jobs granularly one by one, which is time consuming and potentially ineffective.

PowerShell: Get list of timer jobs

```
Get-SPTimerJob
```

PowerShell: Set timer job parameters

```
Set-SPTimerJob -identity <timer job>
```

PowerShell: Disable timer job

```
Disable-SPTimerJob
```

PowerShell: Enable timer job

```
Enable-SPTimerJob
```

More info

Adding a new timer job is not a function of maintenance. The reason for a timer job to be added is due to a new functional business requirement that requires a scheduled task. There is not a single PowerShell command or function in the Central Administration that creates a timer job.

The creation of a new timer job must be done through code via a solution package.

See also

▸ *Running a timer job on demand*

Running a timer job on demand

Sometimes it is necessary to run a timer job immediately. The reasons for this are varied. It may need to be done due to the fact the job failed previously. The administrator may need to do it based on a business process dependency.

This recipe shows how to run a timer job immediately.

Getting ready

You must have farm-level administrative permissions to the Central Administration site.

How to do it...

1. Open the SharePoint 2010 Central Administration website.
2. Click **Monitoring**. Under the second section named **Timer Jobs**, click **Check Job Status**.
3. There are three sections: **Scheduled**, **Running**, and **History**. Click on the time job you wish to run.

4. We have chosen the **Immediate Alerts** option and here is the resulting form:

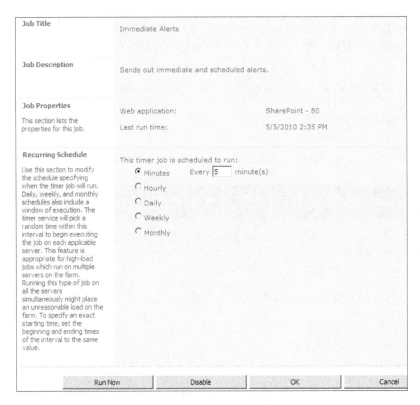

5. Click on the **Run Now** button.

How it works...

The Windows SharePoint Services Timer (SPTimerV4) service is used to run SharePoint 2010 tasks. If this is not running, none of the timer jobs will run.

The timer job executes under OWSTIMER.exe, which is the executable for SPTimerV4.

There's more...

PowerShell can be used instead of Central Administration to immediately start a timer job.

PowerShell: Start a Timer Job

```
Start-SPTimerJob -identity <timer job>
```

See also

▸ *Timer job management*

Configuring Sandbox functionality

The term Sandbox brings to mind a research and development paradigm in the minds of most of the technical folks. A **Sandbox** is typically a physically separate testing area where developers can implement different code configurations without affecting production. The Sandbox is seen as an area to unit test the development code. Only when it has passed with zero defects, is it moved into a production environment where it will be tested on a system.

SharePoint 2010 has an infrastructure component called the Sandbox. The intent of this component is to provide developers with an area to deploy code that is managed and will not adversely affect the associated web application. The Sandbox addresses the pain organizations have to face when deploying code that is fully trusted and must be managed in some manner by the Farm Administrator.

The Sandbox is physically tied to the production box. Code within the Sandbox is running in production.

Solutions deployed to the Sandbox are partially trusted. These solutions run with a subset of the SharePoint object model. A Site Collection Administrator is able to implement these solutions and define a containment area. Administrators define the containment.

This recipe shows how to implement Sandbox functionality in a farm.

Getting ready

You must be a server administrator in order to start a service through the service's Microsoft Management Console (MMC).

You must have farm-level administrative permissions to the Central Administration site.

How to do it...

1. On the web front-end, click **Start**. Navigate to **Administrative Tools**, and click **Services**. The following screenshot appears. It must be enabled to be operational.

Windows SharePoint Services User Code Host V4	Executes user code in a sandbox	Disabled

2. Once enabled, close the **Services** dialog.

3. Open the SharePoint 2010 Central Administration website.

4. Click **System Settings**. Under **Servers**, click **Manage services on server**.

5. Click **Start** on the **Microsoft SharePoint Foundation User Code Service**, as shown in the following screenshot:

Microsoft SharePoint Foundation User Code Service	Stopped	Start

How it works...

Sandbox functionality is a separate process that integrates with web applications. While IIS runs application solutions (DLLs) in W3WP.exe, the Sandbox runs these solutions in three different processes.

▶ SPUCHostService.exe

▶ SPUCWorkerProcess.exe

▶ SPUCWorkerProcessProxy.exe

This isolates the Sandbox solution so that it does not adversely affect the web application and farm. The code installed into the Sandbox is managed by a Site Collection Administrator. The Site Collection Administrator can handle uploading and enabling these solutions and monitoring their resource usage. The positive effect of this is that the Farm Administrator is now focused on farm resources and tasks.

4

Site Administration

In this chapter, we will cover:

- ▶ Migrating a site collection
- ▶ Provisioning a site via Windows PowerShell
- ▶ Managing the Term Store
- ▶ Adding a column with property of managed metadata
- ▶ Setting up a site collection policy
- ▶ Configuring a document set
- ▶ Configuring multiple Send To connections
- ▶ Setting up an enterprise wiki

Introduction

Microsoft is making a conscious effort to push the task of site administration out of the realm of IT administrator. Organizations can be decentralized and become agile if the ability to do more comes closer to the front lines. Yet, organizations still need to retain central control and ensure the integrity of their SharePoint Farm solutions.

The Sandbox functionality in SharePoint 2010 is an example of a win-win solution. IT retains central control of the farm, the hardware, and provides limits. IT administrators can designate a power user who has the ability to roll out code for their SharePoint instance, without adversely affecting the entire farm.

Many modifications can be done at the site collection level by power users. These modifications have ramifications across the entire organization. Here is a simple clarification of the terms site and site collection:

- ▶ **Site Collection**: This is a hierarchical collection of sites that has a single top-level site.
- ▶ **Subsite**: A subsite is a single SharePoint site within a site collection. It inherits its properties, such as navigation and security, from the top-level site.

Site collections are beneficial as they promote standardization and automation. By automation, we mean that the modifications do not have to be applied to every child site; they are inherited.

Some site collection-level modifications require configuration in Central Administration.

In this chapter, we will see some of the common tasks that are done from a site collection administration level. All of the recipes are related to promoting collaboration and common standards at a site collection level. This means when implemented, the recipes can be repeated and extended throughout the SharePoint Farm.

Migrating a site collection

Moving a site collection to another content database is a task that is incumbent upon a SharePoint Farm Administrator. There are several reasons why this may need to be done:

- ▶ We may need to combine several site collections under one content database
- ▶ The site collection is getting too large and must be moved to new content database

This is going to be shown via PowerShell. The strength of this method is that it facilitates the scripting of tasks that are considered repetitive. In this way, administrators can create scripts to move more than one site collection at a time.

Getting ready

User must have access to one of the servers running PowerShell 2.0 and should be a member of the WSS_ADMIN_WPG on the local computer. User must also be a member of the db_owner database role and the SharePoint_Shell_Access role in the following databases:

- ▶ Source content database
- ▶ Administration content database
- ▶ Destination content database
- ▶ Configuration database

There must be an existing site collection that is going to be moved. In addition, a destination content database must be set up within a web application, prior to performing this recipe.

For this recipe to work, the content database and the site collection must be on the same SQL server and in the same web application.

How to do it...

1. Click on the **Start** button on the web front-end.
2. Under **All Programs**, navigate to the `Microsoft SharePoint 2010 Products` folder.
3. Right-click **SharePoint 2010 Management Shell** and select the **Run as Administrator** option. The PowerShell console will appear.
4. Type in the following command into the console window:

   ```
   Move-SPSite –identity <site collection URL> -destinationdatabase
   <content database>
   ```

   Press the *Enter* key.

5. A prompt will appear asking for confirmation. It will look similar to the following:

   ```
   PS C:\Users\Administrator> move-spsite –identity http://2008server/sites/mtsite
   –destinationdatabase wss_content_1

   Confirm
   Are you sure you want to perform this action?
   Performing operation "Move-SPSite" on Target "http://2008server/sites/mtsite".
   [Y] Yes  [A] Yes to All  [N] No  [L] No to All  [S] Suspend  [?] Help
   (default is "Y"):Y
   WARNING: IIS must be restarted before this change will take effect. To restart
   IIS, open a command prompt window and type iisreset.
   ```

   Type in *Y* and press the *Enter* key.

6. Perform an `iisreset` operation in the command prompt window.

How it works...

PowerShell is a command line scripting language that has access to the SharePoint object model.

In this example under the web application, occupying Port 80, there are two content databases:

- `Wss_content`
- `Wss_content_1`

A site collection named `mtsite` was created under the content database named `wss_content`. The URL is (shown in the preceding figure): `http://2008server/sites/mtsite`.

The site collection was moved via PowerShell to the `wss_content_1` database. Afterwards, an IISRESET was done, which is necessary to implement the change.

There's more...

One of the reasons behind the need to migrate a site collection is its size. The following is a simple PowerShell command to ascertain the size of a site collection:

```
Get-SPSiteAdministration -Identity <site URL> .DiskUsed
```

See also

> ▶ The *Upgrading MOSS 2007 to SharePoint 2010* recipe from Chapter 1, *Upgrading and Configuring SharePoint 2010*

Provisioning a site via Windows PowerShell

PowerShell is a scripting technology that can be used to automate many of the tasks an administrator must perform. It is performed through a console, on the server running PowerShell.

Provisioning sites at enterprise companies is one of those tasks that can be automated. While this can be performed through the Central Administration interface, it is more efficient to perform this task through PowerShell.

This recipe will show how to provision a site collection.

Getting ready

User must have access to one of the servers running PowerShell 2.0 and must be a member of the `WSS_ADMIN_WPG` role on the local computer. User must also be a member of the `db_owner` database role and the `SharePoint_Shell_Access` role in the following databases:

- ▶ Source content database
- ▶ Administration content database
- ▶ Destination Content Database
- ▶ Configuration Database

How to do it...

1. Click on the **Start** button on the web front-end.

2. Under **All Programs**, navigate to the `Microsoft SharePoint 2010 Products` folder.

3. Right-click **SharePoint 2010 Management Shell** and select the **Run as Administrator** option. The PowerShell console will appear.

4. Type in the following commands into the console window, pressing the *Enter* key after each command:

   ```
   $url = "http://2008server/ts"

   $SiteTitle = "Team Site"

   $teamsite = Get-SPWebTemplate "STS#0"

   New-SPSite -URL $url -OwnerAlias domain/username -Template
   $teamsite -name $SiteTitle
   ```

5. You will see the screen confirming that the site has now been created (refer to the next screenshot).

```
PS C:\Users\Administrator> new-spsite -URL $url -owneralias pzs\administrator -t
emplate $teamsite -name $siteTitle

Url
---
http://2008server/sites/ts

PS C:\Users\Administrator>
```

How it works...

This is a very simple PowerShell script that creates a site collection. These scripts can be combined into a `.ps1` file. By doing this, the administrator can automate the creation of sites and utilize parameters or reference an XML file to create multiple sites.

The first line assigns the new site collection URL, `http://2008server/ts`, to the `$url` variable. `Team Site` is the name of the site collection.

`Get-SPWebTemplate` gets all the available SharePoint site templates. `STS#0` is the template for the `Team Site` site collection and is assigned to the `$teamsite` variable.

`New-SPSite` utilizes all the variables and, using a domain account, creates the site collection `ts`. The account will be made the Site Collection Administrator for the newly created site collection.

There's more...

This is only one example of the `New-SPSite` command. However, if you type `Get-help New-SPSite -examples` in the PowerShell console, you are provided with three additional examples.

Typing in `Get-help New-SPSite -full` gives you a brief description of the parameters and notifies you which ones are required.

Managing the Term Store

In *Chapter 2, Service Applications*, we saw how to set up the managed metadata service. Using the Term Store repository, organizations can set up a common vocabulary for the entire organization. Each industry—be it be healthcare, finance, construction, or some other—has its own vernacular.

The Term Store can be leveraged across site collections so as an organization segments its processes, each can use terminology that is common.

With the Term Store, organizations can create a common taxonomy to be leveraged in their SharePoint 2010 implementation.

Getting ready

You must have farm-level administrative permissions to the Central Administration site.

The managed metadata service must be configured and functional. To read more about it, refer to the *Setting up the managed metadata service* recipe in Chapter 2.

How to do it...

1. Open up the SharePoint 2010 Central Administration website.
2. Click **Application Management**.
3. The third section is **Service Applications**. Under it, click **Manage Service applications**.
4. Find the Managed metadata service instance where you have the Term Store that you wish to manage. Hover over the name of the service and click on it.
5. The following screen appears:

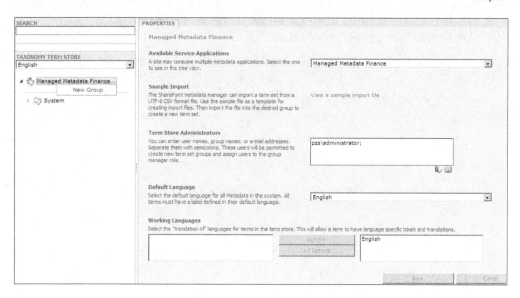

On this screen, we can assign an administrator user, who is a domain-level account, to manage the Term Store. We can also choose the default language. Choose **New Group** under **Managed Metadata Finance** as seen in the preceding screenshot.

6. Name the new group as **Finance.**

7. Create a new term set by clicking the drop-down list adjacent to the **Finance** option. Refer to the next screenshot:

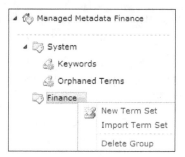

8. Enter the term name as **Business Financial Terms**. We will get the following properties form on the right-hand side:

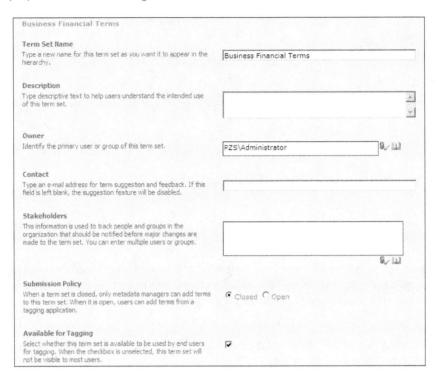

Enter values for the **Description** and **Contact** field, retaining default values for the rest of the fields.

9. Click **Save**.

10. From the drop-down list that appears to the right of the **Business Financial Terms** option, select **Create Term**.

11. Enter **EBITDA**. On the right-hand side will appear the following properties form:

EBITDA

Available for Tagging
Select whether this term is available to be used by end users for tagging. When unselected this term will be visible but not enabled in tagging tools.

☑

Language
Select a language of the labels for the term you would like to edit.

English

Description
Descriptions will help users know when to use this term, and to disambiguate amongst similar terms.

Earnings before interest, taxes, depreciation and amortization. An indicator of a company financial performance.

Default Label
Enter one label as the default for this language.

EBITDA

Other Labels
Enter synonyms and abbreviations for this term. (You can enter a word or phrase per line.)

EBITA
add new label

Member Of

Term Set Name	Term Set Description	Parent Term	Source Term
Business Financial Terms		Business Financial Terms	⊙

In the form, fill in the values for the **Description** and **Other Labels** field, keeping the other fields to their default values.

12. Click **Save**.

How it works...

The Term Store taxonomy is managed in a hierarchical fashion, hence the term taxonomy. At the top of the hierarchy is an object called Group. A **Group** is a security construct for the management of term sets. Each group can have a manager(s) who is/are responsible as the stakeholder(s) of the group. Each Group can also have contributors who are able to edit and add to the term sets and Terms.

The next item in the hierarchy is Term Set. This is a container for Terms and can be imported or created manually as we did in the recipe. Each term set can have an owner. The term sets are organized into groups, which can be based on the business stakeholders. There are a maximum of 1,000 Term Sets per group.

Finally, the last item in the hierarchy are the Terms themselves. Each term may have a synonym, which is an alternate name for the primary term. There is a maximum of 30,000 Terms added to a Term Set. These are added where the **Other Labels** is designated. In the recipe we have just seen, a user can type in **EBITA**, and when the record is saved, **EBITDA** will be shown in the field.

These items, which include managed as well as unmanaged items (keywords, orphaned terms), are saved in the managed metadata database.

There's more...

Manually creating Terms is inefficient and not practical when creating an enterprise information architecture. SharePoint 2010 has the facility to import term sets. In step 7 of this recipe, the screenshot shows a menu item of a function called **Import Term Set**.

The import file must be a comma-separated file that contains a header row. There is a sample of an import file under the managed metadata service. We can see from the screenshot of step 5 that there is a **Sample Import** section included. To the right is a link to a sample file. Use this as your template when creating your own import file.

More info

There is a checkbox for tagging on the properties page of the Terms object. When made available, users can utilize the Terms to tag their documents or SharePoint pages. This gives an organization a consistent view of their information architecture.

The following screenshot shows the type ahead capability when a user enters a managed keyword tagging to an uploaded document:

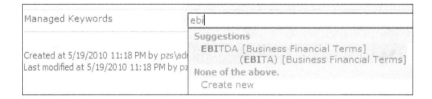

See also

> ▸ Setting up the managed metadata service recipe from *Chapter 2, Service Applications*

Adding a column with the property of Managed Metadata

Managed Metadata gives organizations the capability of using a common terminology across the enterprise. When properly utilized, Managed Metadata will contain the language a company speaks. There are many terms that refer to a base term and Managed Metadata does the work of standardizing the "slang" of a company.

An example of this is the term North America. It is referred to as NA, United States, or Canada. Set up properly, the base term can be NA, but any of the aforementioned terms can be put in by the user.

All of this data is saved in what is called a Term Store. The Term Store as we have seen in previous recipes is a repository where that data is stored and configured.

In order for users to leverage this data, it must be input somewhere at the site level as a function of metadata. This is done via content types, document libraries, and lists.

This recipe will show how to add a managed metadata column in a list.

Getting ready

User must have designer rights to a site. The Managed metadata service for Finance should be configured as described in previous recipes.

How to do it...

1. Navigate to a site with the team site template implemented.
2. In the **Quick Launch** (left-hand side vertical navigation) area, click **Tasks**.
3. At the top is the menu item called **List Tools**.

   Click **List**.
4. The ribbon appears and is lit up. At the far right end of the ribbon is a button called **List Settings**; click on that button.
5. The list information appears. Under the section named **Columns**, click **Create Column**.
6. A form appears with radio buttons for the different types of data. At the bottom of the named types is the radio button named **Managed Metadata**; select that button.

   There are seven sections to the adjusted form. Enter the **Column name** as **Financial Term**.
7. The second section is **Additional Column Settings;** leave it as is.
8. Section three, **Multiple Value field**, allows for multiple values in a column. Do not check the box.
9. Section four is about how to display the value from the term set. There is a radio button named **Display term label in the field**; make sure it is selected.

10. In the section number five, we pick the value from the term set. Enter **ebi** into the text box under the **Use a managed term set** option and click the binoculars icon. You should see the following screenshot:

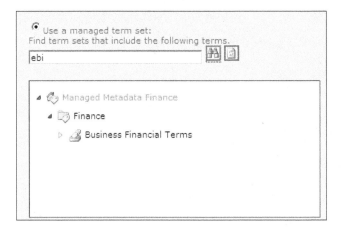

11. Click **Business Financial Terms** and then click **OK** at the bottom of the form.

How it works...

Business Financial Terms is the Term Set being employed with this column we called Financial Term. We have assigned this column to the list called Tasks. Any time a task is entered, a financial term can be associated with this task.

In the example that we have shown, we are consuming the Managed Metadata Finance Service Application. The screenshot shows **ebi**, but with the type-ahead functionality, EBITDA will be populated. We can add other financial terms such as assets, cashflow, cost of sales, and so on. As long as they are in the term set, every task can be related to one of these terms.

Across an enterprise organization, a controller can find all of the tasks that are directly related to finance.

There's more...

When a task is being entered, and one of the fields is of the type Managed Metadata, there is a "type-ahead suggestions" service available as we saw in the last recipe. Included in the suggestions are synonyms that have been defined in the Term Store.

This feature helps companies standardize the language of their business. Consider a small example. Regions is a popular metadata term. Large international companies have regions set up to fit their businesses. For one company, the North America region may consist of the United States, Canada, and Mexico, whereas for some other, the North America region might constitute United States and Canada.

By correctly setting up the metadata in the Term Store, a user only has to type in Mexico and the region will be automatically populated. The following screenshot shows the same concept with **EBITDA**.

See also

▸ *Setting up the managed metadata service* from *Chapter 2, Service Applications*

Setting up a site collection policy

Policy is a term to which people have an immediate reaction. Speaking of policy immediately reminds us of governance, rules, and enforcement. When dealing with an organization's data, having a policy in place is a positive thing.

Take the example of a publicly traded company. It is subject to audits, investor relations, not to mention Sarbanes-Oxley regulations. Data must be accounted for and properly managed.

The term policy in this context refers to management of information through a policy. In SharePoint terms, a policy is a set of rules that are applied against content types, document sets, folders, or document libraries. This set of rules governs the content, and tells the system what action(s) to take against the content, based on some type of status.

Creating site collection policies gives an organization the ability to standardize their policies. As sites are created under the root site, they inherit the policies.

The policies can be exported by an administrator and imported into other site collections.

In this recipe we are going to create a site collection policy and associate it with a content type.

Getting ready

There are two prerequisites:

▸ You must be a Site Collection Administrator
▸ There must be a custom content type created prior to doing this recipe

How to do it...

1. Navigate to a site with the team site template implemented.

2. Click on the drop-down icon next to **Site Actions** and then click **Site Settings**.

3. Under the category **Site Collection Administration**, click **Site collection policies**.

4. Click **Create**. A form appears that needs to be filled out.

5. Give name to the policy and write some description about it.

   ❑ **Name: Cookbook SC Policy**

   ❑ **Description**: The cookbook site collection policy enables auditing on an object to determine who is downloading, moving, or copying documents

6. Enter a **Policy Statement**.

7. There are four check boxes: **Enable Retention**, **Enable Auditing**, **Enable Barcodes**, and **Enable Labels**. Check the box for **Auditing**. Then check the remaining boxes as seen in the following screenshot:

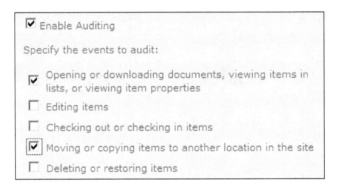

   Click **OK**.

8. Click on dropdown next to **Site Actions**, and then click **Site Settings**.

9. Under the **Galleries** section, click **Site content types**.

10. Choose the custom content type that has been created prior to performing this recipe.

11. Click **Information management policy settings**.

12. The **Specify the Policy** form appears. Choose the radio button as seen in the following screen:

Specify the Policy

Specify the information management policy for this content type. If you would like to use one of this site's predefined policies then select "Use a site policy". Alternatively, you can directly create or edit the policy settings.

Specify the policy:

○ None

○ Define a policy...

◉ Use a site collection policy:

[Cookbook SC Policy ▾]

Description:
The cookbook site collection policy enables auditing on an object to determine who is downloading, moving, or copying documents.

13. Click **OK**.

How it works...

Steps 1 to 7 help set up a policy at the site collection level. The policy is now available to be applied against an object.

In steps 8 to 13, we apply the policy named Cookbook SC Policy against a custom content type that was created prior to this recipe. If you try to associate a site collection policy with an out of the box content type, you cannot do it. The option is not there.

The policy we created audits when an item is moved, copied, or downloaded. This gives the reviewer, the ability to know who is doing what with the objects that belong to the content type. Every item that has been assigned the custom content type will inherit the applied policy.

For instance, if the content type you created inherits from the Document Content type, every document in the library has audits performed on it.

There's more...

The Site Collection Administrator can also restrict the ability to create a policy on a content type or library. This means the people who are creating content types or libraries can use a policy only from the site collection policies gallery.

Configuring a Document Set

A document set allows an organization to collect related documents and group them together. When grouping the related documents together, they can be treated as one when it comes to metadata, workflow, versioning, and compliance.

For example, a document set for obtaining a mortgage loan can consist of the following forms—credit application, asset list, employment history, deed, and sales contract.

When buying a house, there are many forms to be filled out. They are methodically handled by several different parties—the bank, the seller, the real estate company, and so on. It all starts with a mortgage application. The application is submitted and a workflow kicks off for each item such as getting a credit report, appraisal on the property, employment verification, among other things.

Once the individual workflows come back with information, the application is then submitted to another party, which must approve the loan. Each workflow item is kicked off independently, but together they contribute to the final answer, which is whether or not the mortgage is approved for the potential buyer.

Once the mortgage is approved, there is a deed issued and sent to a title company and a payment plan is set up. This process is comprised of many forms and parties, and your ability to get the final approval is contingent upon each step being completed properly.

This recipe will show how to set up a document set for the mortgage process.

Getting ready

We first need to enable the Document Set Site Collection Feature.

Set up the following content types and group them under the type *Mortgage*:

- `AssetListCT`—parent content type of Item
- `CreditApplicationCT`—parent content type of Document
- `SalesContractCT`—parent content type of Document

How to do it...

1. Navigate to a site with the team site template implemented.
2. Click on the dropdown next to **Site Actions**, and then click **Site Settings**.
3. Under the category named **Galleries**, click **Site content types**.
4. Click **Create**. The following form appears:

5. Fill in the form as shown in previous screenshot and then click **OK**.

6. Click **Document Set Settings**.

7. Under the **Allowed Content Types** section, choose **Mortgage** from the drop-down list. Select **CreditApplicationCT** and **SalesContractCT** from under the **Content Type** dropdown.

8. In Default Content, choose each content type selected in step 7 and add an associated document for each. Check the **Add the name of the Document Set to each file name** box. Your screen should look like the following screenshot:

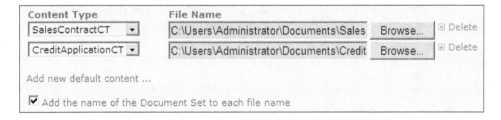

9. Under Shared Columns, check the boxes for **Description** and **Managed Keywords**.

10. Add **Managed Keywords** to the **Welcome Page Columns**.

11. Do not customize the **Welcome** page.

12. Leave the **Update all content types inheriting from this type** option to **Yes**. Click **OK**.

13. Create a document library called Mortgage.

14. The ribbon lights up. At the far end, click **Library Settings**.

15. Click **Advanced Settings**.

16. Set the **Allow management of content types** option to **Yes**. Click **OK**.

17. In the **Content Types** section, click **Add from existing site content types**.

18. Add the MortgageDS content type, and click **OK**.

19. Navigate back to the Mortgage document library. Click **Documents** under **Library Tools**.

20. Click the drop-down list next to **New Document** and select MortgageDS.

21. An entry form appears. Fill in the **Name, Description,** and **Managed Keywords** fields. Click **Save**.

22. The following landing page appears with the necessary documents:

How it works...

Steps 1 to 5 show the process of creating a document set and giving it a name. Document Set is a content type. In our example, `MortageDS` inherits from this content type.

In steps 6 to 13, content types are assigned to be part of the document set. Also, documents are associated with their content types in step 8. In step 9, columns are included in the welcome page. These columns can be shared across the document in the document set itself. For instance, we could have added Mortgage Company as a column and had it applied to each document in the set.

This recipe did not set up any custom columns. Also, this recipe did not customize the welcome page.

The last part of the recipe is creating the document library, enabling management of content types, and then assigning the Mortgage document set to the library. When a new document set is created, all the associated documents with their content types are shown.

A loan processor could now go through and process all the necessary paper work without missing a mandatory form.

There's more...

Workflows can be created with SharePoint Designer and applied to the entire document set. Keeping in mind our Mortgage loan example, a workflow could be set up to send information to the title company and get information from the credit bureau. The application could then be sent to the bank after the credit bureau sends their information.

In addition, permission levels can be set on the individual documents. Finally, retention policies can be added to the document set.

More info

Document sets are built upon the content type `SPFolder`.

See also

- ▶ *Setting up Retention Management*

Configuring multiple Send To connections

Records management is the careful management of information for an entire lifecycle. This includes how documents are routed and referenced.

A records management feature that deserves its own recipe is the ability to set up multiple Send To connections. What is meant by this capability is the functionality to route a document to multiple areas in a site. The reasoning for this is varied.

There may be a Request for Quote (RFQ) that comes in and needs to go to several folks upon being uploaded into the system, as each individual may have a role in a particular part of the document.

Another use case is when an asset must have one source location but must be in several other locations. Thus, links are established to one source.

Farm administrators have the ability to define multiple locations where a record can be routed. Not only can an administrator specify the connections, but they can define how that record is manipulated. Is it copied? Is it moved? Moved with a link to the source?

In this recipe, multiple connections will be set up in Central Administration. We will also see how this affects the consumer of the site.

Getting ready

You must have farm-level administrative permissions to the Central Administration site.

This recipe builds upon the previous recipe on document set creation. You will need to create two Records Center sites if you have not performed the previous recipe:

- **Mortgage Active**: `http://2008server/sites/ts/MortgagesActive`
- **Mortgages Archived**: `http://2008server/sites/ts/MortgageRepository`

How to do it...

1. Open the SharePoint 2010 Central Administration website.
2. Click **General Application Settings**.
3. Under the **External Service Connections** section, click **Configure send to connections**.
4. The following form appears:

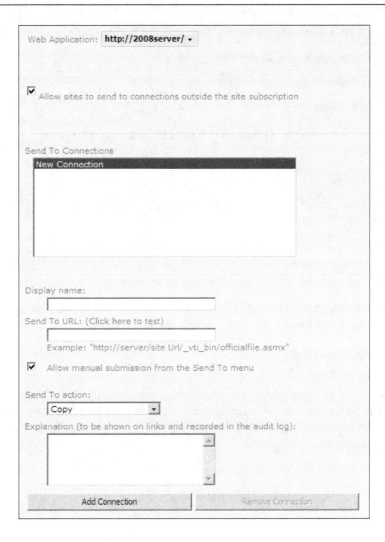

Ensure this is being done under the proper web application.

Keep the check on the box for allowing sites to send to connections outside of the site subscription. Fill in the following details:

- **Display Name: Active Mortgages**
- **Send To URL**: http://2008server/sites/ts/MortgagesActive
- Check the **Allow manual submission from the Send To Menu** option
- **Send To action:** Select the **Move and keep link** option from the drop-down list
- Enter an **Explanation**.

Click **Add Connection.**

5. Perform the same steps as step 4, changing the following:

    - ❑ **Display Name: Archive Mortgages**
    - ❑ **Send To URL**: `http://2008server/sites/ts/MortgageRepository`

    Click **Add Connection**.

There should be two connections showing in the **Send To Connections** box.

How it works...

The Send To connection is configured per web application and is available to all records in that container.

From the screenshot of step 4, we can see there is a **Send To URL** option. When the URL is entered and tested, it is verified as successful via the `officialfile.asmx` web service. If it cannot route to the URL provided, it will return an error message.

There are three different actions that can be implemented when routing a record, of which the recipe utilized **Move and Keep Link**. There is also **Move** and **Copy**.

There's more...

Once the Send To is configured, the users with the proper rights can go to a record and choose **Send To other location**. In the previous recipe, we created a mortgage dataset and populated it with one record called **Peter Serzo**.

From the preceding screenshot, click **Send To other location** and the following form appears, showing us the available locations to choose from:

Once the `Send` command is initiated, the prescribed action is taken.

See also

▸   *Configuring a document set*

Setting up an enterprise wiki

An **enterprise wiki** is an efficient way to share knowledge across an organization. The wiki is an organic self-policing site for knowledge. In addition, the users who are consuming the site will categorize objects and the site will contain its own taxonomy.

In reality, it is an online database that promotes collaboration in an organization. SharePoint 2010 contains this functionality out of the box and includes a few bells and whistles such as:

▸   Tagging

▸   Comments

▸   Ratings

▸   Managed metadata

For some of the additional functionality to work, a managed metadata service should be set up and configured.

In this recipe, we will set up an Enterprise Wiki at the Site Collection level.

Getting ready

You must have farm-level administrative permissions to the Central Administration site.

How to do it...

1. Open the SharePoint 2010 Central Administration website.
2. Click **Application Management**.
3. Under the **Site Collections** section, click **Create site collections**.
4. Ensure that the proper **Web Application** is chosen.
5. Enter **Cookbook Wiki** as the **Title**.
6. Enter **CW** as the **URL**.

7. In the **Select a Template** section, choose the **Publishing tab** and then click **Enterprise Wiki**. Refer to the following screenshot:

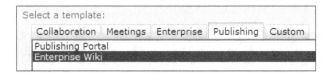

8. Enter the value for the **Primary Site Collection Administrator**.

9. Click **OK**.

How it works...

The enterprise wiki is a publishing site. For its infrastructure, we can use all of the components that are contained within. Web parts such as the powerful Content Query or media web part are available. Lists, pictures, or even data from external sources can be leveraged and surfaced.

The ribbon exposes the previously mentioned items and also the rich text editor. The publishing infrastructure contains templates so that an editor can change the layout by selecting an item from the **Page Layout** tab.

The SharePoint 2010 Enterprise Wiki Page is a content type that includes the following columns:

Name	File
Title	Single line of text
Comments	Multiple lines of text
Contact	Person or Group
Contact E-Mail Address	Single line of text
Contact Name	Single line of text
Contact Picture	Hyperlink or Picture
Rollup Image	Publishing Image
Target Audiences	Audience Targeting
Page Content	Publishing HTML
Rating (0-5)	Rating (0-5)
Number of Ratings	Number of Ratings
Wiki Categories	Managed Metadata
Managed Keywords	Managed Metadata

The wiki that comes with SharePoint Foundation is derived from the document content type. It does not include items such as **Target Audiences** and **Rating**. It is an extremely light version.

There's more...

PowerShell can be used to create the Wiki site. Also, the Wiki site does not have to be created at the Site Collection level and can be a subsite of another site.

```
New-SPSite http://site.com/EnterpriseWiki -OwnerAlias <domain/user>
-Template "ENTERWIKI#0"
```

More info

When the SharePoint 2010 Enterprise Wiki site collection was added, a group was created in the Managed Metadata Term Store. Within the group, we can create a Term Set and some Terms.

Now when we edit a page in our wiki and assign a category, we can categorize our pages across the organization in a standard way. Refer to the following screenshot:

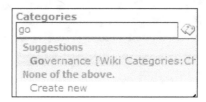

See also

▶ The *Setting up the managed metadata service* recipe from *Chapter 2, Service Applications*

5
Monitoring and Reporting

In this chapter, we will cover:

- ▶ Accessing the SharePoint 2010 logging database
- ▶ Configuring what gets logged
- ▶ Editing rule definitions in the health analyzer
- ▶ Viewing web analytics reports
- ▶ Troubleshooting with correlation IDs
- ▶ Enabling the Developer Dashboard

Introduction

SharePoint 2010 has been architected to be a proactive system that provides many tools to the administrators. The goal is to catch issues before they occur. If they do occur, the system should give the administrator the capability to debug the issues with the least amount of resistance.

One example of this is the new logging database. It collects information from disparate servers and collates this information into the database. For instance, the **Unified Logging Service** (**ULS**) logs collect information that is useful in troubleshooting issues. These logs are found on every SharePoint Server. These ULS logs are collected from all servers and the event logs. This makes the logging database a valuable tool. It is must-have knowledge for SharePoint administrators and covered in one of the recipes.

Reporting is another area where SharePoint 2010 has been given focus. Reports are more robust and present better information down at the site level. This gives administrators a better idea about how their site is being utilized, what they are searching for, and uncovers where functionality is lacking.

When it comes to monitoring and being proactive, SharePoint offers another level of service — self-correcting health monitoring. SharePoint 2010 health monitoring jobs have the ability to uncover issues, report them, and then SharePoint is able to automatically correct the issue (in some cases).

Finally, SharePoint 2010 delivers a tool that can give details on the performance of a page. Currently, we have to use a tool such as Microsoft Visual Round Trip Analyzer. This is now an innate built-in capability of the infrastructure. The last recipe in this chapter shows how to use this tool.

The monitoring and reporting capabilities combined together empower the administrator to be proactive with regards to the health of the SharePoint farm. These capabilities can be leveraged with other SharePoint functions such as alerts, so that the team managing the SharePoint farm should be well versed in the performance of the installation.

Accessing the SharePoint 2010 logging database

As mentioned in the introduction, the SharePoint 2010 logging database is a major enhancement to monitoring, debugging, and protecting the health of the farm.

By default, the database is called `WSS_Logging`. This database should be the starting point for administrators to collect and analyze information.

In this recipe, we will access the database and run a view (that already is installed) against it.

Getting ready

You must have farm-level administrative permissions to the Central Administration site. You must have read and execute permissions as well to the `WSS_Logging` database in order to open and execute views.

How to do it...

1. Open up SQL Server Management Studio.
2. When asked for authentication, log in to the correct instance where SharePoint is running using your windows authentication credentials. If SQL authentication is the preferred method of connecting, use the appropriate User ID/Password.

3. Navigate to the `WSS_Logging` database and click on the plus sign to expand it.

4. Under the toolbar at the top, click on the **New Query** button.

5. In the new query window, type in the following query: `Select * from RequestUsage`.

6. Click **Execute**. Results are populated in the window pane below the query, as seen in the following screenshot:

How it works...

In the above recipe a view called `RequestUsage` was executed. This is an out of the box view that provides site usage information. It provides information such as the referring URL, the browser being used, the site ID, the web ID, the server URL, the request type, and when it was done.

The logging database contains, but is not limited to, the following information:

ULS logs	NT event logs	Performance counters
Feature usage	Blocking queries	Site usage
Timer job information		

It is a place where information is aggregated from across the farm. For instance, all ULS logs, from every SharePoint server, are collected within this database.

There are 26 views installed by default. However, the purpose of this database is to give administrators and developers a place to log information based on processes. These are typically custom processes. Views can be created to meet an organization's needs.

There's more...

The location of the logging database is not a setting that can be done through the user interface in Central Administration. Because of all the data that is collected in this database, it can grow quite large. Additionally, as SharePoint-integrated applications are created, developers can utilize this database to communicate issues.

Therefore, due to size and usage, it is a wise idea to move the database to another physical location such as a dedicated disk. This can be done only via PowerShell, using the following command:

```
Set-SPUsageApplication -DatabaseServer <DB Server Name> -DatabaseName
<DB Name> [-DatabaseUsername <User Name>] [-DatabasePassword <Password>]
```

More info

The ULS logs are present on every WFE. It is important for an Administrator to know where to find these logs manually. They are located at the following location: `\Common Files\ Microsoft Shared\Web Server Extensions\14\Logs`.

See also

▶ *Configuring what gets logged*

Configuring what gets logged

The SharePoint 2010 logging database covered in the previous recipe captures information that can be modified via the Central Administration interface. The advantage of this being that the collection of information can be voluminous, which can also be the disadvantage.

Disk space, I/O, and just the amount of data needed to retain this information can become an issue. Being able to reduce the type of information that gets captured is critical to the wellness of your farm.

In this recipe, we will cover how to change what gets captured and put into the logging database.

Getting ready

You must have farm-level administrative permissions to the Central Administration site.

How to do it...

1. Open the SharePoint 2010 Central Administration website.
2. Click **Monitoring**.
3. Under the **Reporting** section, click **Configure usage and health data collection**.
4. The following form appears for configuration:

Usage data collection

Usage data collection will log events whenever various events occur in your SharePoint deployment. Usage Logging enables analysis and reporting, but also uses system resources and can impact performance and disk usage.

☑ Enable usage data collection

Event Selection

Logging enables analysis and reporting, but also uses system resources and can impact performance and disk usage. Only log those events for which you want regular reports.

For sporadic reports or investigations, consider turning on logging for specific events and then disabling logging for these events after the report or investigation is complete.

Events to log:
- ☑ Content Import Usage
- ☑ Content Export Usage
- ☑ Page Requests
- ☑ Feature Use
- ☑ Search Query Usage
- ☑ Site Inventory Usage
- ☑ Timer Jobs
- ☑ Rating Usage

Usage data collection settings

Usage logs must be saved in a location that exists on all servers in the farm. Adjust the maximum size to ensure that sufficient disk space is available.

Log file location:
`C:\Program Files\Common Files\Microsoft Shared\Web Server Extensions\14\LOGS\`

Maximum log file size:
`5` GB

Health data collection

Health reports are built by taking snap shots of various resources, data, and processes at specific points in time.

Each element of the health logging system can be individual scheduled.

☑ Enable health data collection

Click the link below to edit the health logging schedule.
Health Logging Schedule

Log Collection Schedule

A time job collects log files from each server and copies events into a database that is used for reporting.

Log collection is required to support reporting, but the timer job can be scheduled based on the requirements and load patterns of your servers.

Click the link below to edit the log collection schedule.
Log Collection Schedule

Fill in the following details:

- **Usage Data Collection**: This is enabled by default.
- **Event Selection**: These are specific events that are being logged. Use the check box to enable or disable them.
- **Usage data collection settings**: In this section, the location of the ULS logs are set. Also, there is a setting to limit the size of the log file.
- **Health data collection**: This is enabled by default.
- **Log Collection Schedule**: Administrator has the ability to change the schedule.

5. Modify the settings in step 4 and click **OK**.

How it works...

The options presented in the usage and health data collection are logged to the logging database and to the ULS logs.

The health logging schedule can be modified to fit the needs (also known as Service Level Agreements) of your organization. It is important to remember that there is a hidden cost associated with the increased logging. The hidden cost is mainly in the form of storage and possibly performance.

The ULS logs have the potential to grow large. The logs can be moved to a new physical location (physical spindle), which does not contain the operating system or WFE/Application server software. The physical location reference must exist on all servers in the farm.

The location of the logs is set within Central Administration. To access the setting, go to Central Administration, click **Monitoring**, and then select **Configure diagnostic logging**. Under the **Trace Log** section is the **Path**. This contains the location of the ULS logs.

There's more...

The logging information is retained for a period of 14 days by default. Using PowerShell you can change this parameter, using the following command:

```
Set-SPUsageDefinition -Identity <GUID> [-Enable] -DaysRetained 14
```

See also

▸ *Accessing the SharePoint 2010 logging database*

Editing rule definitions in the health analyzer

SharePoint 2010 has a built-in health analyzer that acts as a best practice analyzer. The health analyzer will report whether or not the farm is compliant with each predefined health rule. The health analyzer builds upon the best practice analyzer from Microsoft Office SharePoint Server 2007.

There are roughly 65 rules that are categorized as follows:

- ▶ Security
- ▶ Performance
- ▶ Configuration
- ▶ Availability

Each rule is run by a timer job, and each rule has a specific purpose such as checking application pool memory, checking how security is configured on the farm, or checking drive space.

In Central Administration, it is possible to edit existing rules in order to meet the needs of your organization. Changes can be made to the scheduled execution of the job. On the ribbon, there is an option named **Run Now** that will execute the rule immediately. The rules are available out of the box and are meant to allow you to be proactive.

In this recipe, we will modify one of the existing health analyzer rules.

Getting ready

You must have farm-level administrative permissions to the Central Administration site.

How to do it...

1. Open the SharePoint 2010 Central Administration website.
2. Click **Monitoring**.
3. Under the **Health Analyzer** section, click **Review rule definitions**.
4. Under the category **Security**, click **The server farm account should not be used for other services.**

⊟ Category : **Security** (4)

    Accounts used by application pools or service identities are in the local machine Administrators group.

    Web Applications using Claims authentication require an update.

    The server farm account should not be used for other services.

5. A form pops up, which contains the parameter of the rule. The left-most ribbon button is **Edit Item**; click the button. The following screenshot appears:

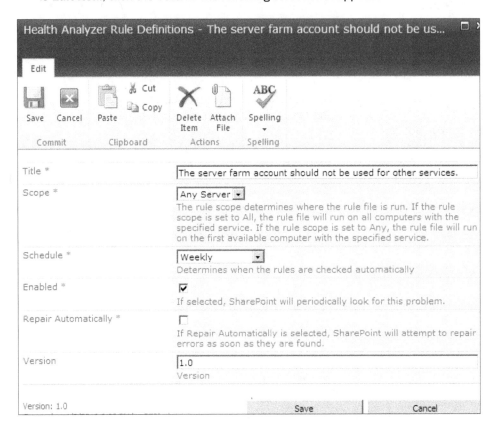

6. Change the **Schedule** to **Daily**, from the default value of **Weekly**.

7. You must also manually change the value of the parameter **Version**. Change it to **2.0**, from present **1.0**.

8. Click **Save**.

How it works...

The health analyzer rule definitions are run via the timer jobs. There are several parameters that the administrator can modify:

▸ **Title**: This is the text description of the rule.

▸ **Scope**: This is where the rule will run.

▸ **Schedule**: This is how often the rules are employed.

▸ **Enabled**: This designates the rule as active.

- ▸ **Repair Automatically**: When the timer job kicks off, it will check the rules. If the rule can be checked and then corrected via SharePoint best practices, it will be.
- ▸ **Version**: This is a manually edited text box that tracks versioning of the rules.

The page also notes who created the rule, and when the rule was last edited and by who.

There's more...

In addition to being able to edit the rule, there are several other parameters as shown by the following screenshot:

- ▸ **Version History**: Shows all the versions
- ▸ **Alert Me**: This notifies you when changes are made
- ▸ **Run Now**: This executes the rule

More info—adding a new health rule

Every rule that a farm installation may need cannot be covered by the out of the box health rules. For instance, consider monitoring the number of tenants in the user profile social database. There may be a need for a governance rule that monitors this and flags the administrator when certain levels are reached; however, there is no out of the box rule available today that can help govern this.

In order to implement a new health rule, code must be written to utilize the `Microsoft.SharePoint.Administration.Health` namespace. Once the assembly is written, it must be placed in the **Global Assembly Cache** (**GAC**) on every machine. The new health rule must then be registered with the SharePoint Health Analyzer. The best way to do this is to create a SharePoint feature that can be activated and deactivated.

Viewing web analytics reports

Web analytics reports are an innate part of the SharePoint 2010 installation. These reports are prebuilt. They use collected data from the active SharePoint installation to present information such as number of site collections, top destinations, top pages, page views, and top referrers. Using this information, an administrator can determine the flow of traffic. This is information that will comprise part of the story for performance monitoring.

This recipe shows how to invoke the reports and how to view custom reports.

Getting ready

You must have farm-level administrative permissions to the Central Administration site.

How to do it...

1. Open up the SharePoint 2010 Central Administration website.
2. Click **Monitoring**.
3. Under the **Reporting** section, click **View Web Analytics reports**.
4. Choose a web application by clicking on it.
5. The page that is presented contains a left-hand navigation, as shown here:

> Summary
>
> Traffic
>
> Number of Page Views
>
> Number of Daily Unique Visitors
>
> Number of Referrers
>
> Top Pages
>
> Top Visitors
>
> Top Referrers
>
> Top Destinations
>
> Top Browsers
>
>
> Search
>
> Number of Queries
>
>
> Inventory
>
> Number of Site Collections
>
> Top Site Collection Templates
>
>
> Customized Reports

Click any of the above options and you will be presented with the appropriate report. When the report is presented, it is shown as a graph at the top and a grid at the bottom.

How it works...

The reporting data is collected by the usage data per web application, per site collection, per site, and finally, per search service application. The web analytics timer job runs as per its schedule and updates the collected information. This recipe showed how to access the reports through Central Administration. They can also be accessed through the site collection and sites via the **Site Actions** drop-down list.

Web analytics is now part of the services infrastructure. It is called the **Web Analytics Service Application**. This must be provisioned and configured similar to setting up the other services, as described in *Chapter 2, Service Applications*.

The following diagram shows the infrastructure components of the Web Analytics Service Application:

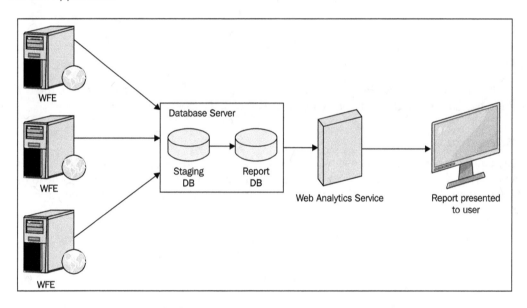

The information is collected on the web front-end (WFE) servers into .usage files. Timer jobs kick off a process that pulls the information into a staging database, where information is kept for 24 hours. Information is then aggregated into the reporting database, where it is retained for a period of 25 months by default.

There's more...

The data shown with date ranges can be modified. This can be achieved by clicking on the **Change Settings** link above the graph:

Date Range 5/9/2010 - 6/7/2010 (UTC-05:00) Eastern Time (US and Canada) Change Settings

The following ribbon appears:

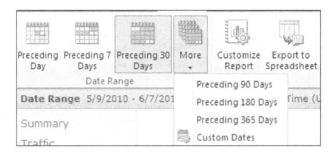

With a click of the appropriate date button, the data will be filtered. Depending on the report, there may be filters other than date.

Finally, the report can also be customized or exported to Excel. This can be done with the help of the two buttons on the right-most side of the preceding screenshot.

More info

Customized reports are also possible. There is an Administrative Report Library in Central Administration. There are folders in that library that contain reports written by someone in the organization. These reports may be particular to an organization's needs or audit concerns, among other things.

There is a **Customized Reports** link on the left-hand navigation shown in a preceding screenshot; currently, there is only Search Administration Reports in there.

See also

  ▶ *Chapter 2, Service Applications*, shows how to set up several different service applications. While Web Analytics are not covered, the basics are the same.

Troubleshooting with correlation IDs

An undesirable thing for users of SharePoint is getting an indefinite message that has a big red "X" and the word "Error" in bold adjacent to it. The user has done something but the page does not tell what the error is and how to fix this error. It only points them to the site administrator, that is, you.

SharePoint 2010 has addressed this issue by creating a mechanism to track communications between the web front-ends and the user's requests. This is in the form of a GUID called the **correlation ID**. Now when a user gets his/her error page, he/she can contact the administrator and provide the correlation ID. The administrator can then track the cause of this error using the correlation ID as a reference in the ULS logs.

This recipe shows the steps to perform after the correlation ID is provided to the administrator. To induce the error with a correlation ID, we will stop the web analytics service.

Getting ready

You must have farm-level administrative permissions to the Central Administration site.

This recipe uses PowerShell. You must be a member of the `SharePoint_Shell_Access` database role on the configuration database. You also must be a member of the `WSS_ADMIN_WPG` local group.

How to do it...

1. In Central Administration, navigate to **System Settings**. Under **Servers**, click **Manage services on server**.
2. Click **Stop** associated with **Web Analytics Web Service**.
3. Click **Monitoring** on the left-hand side navigation.
4. Under **Reporting**, click **View Web Analytics reports**. The following error should be shown:

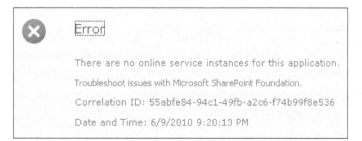

5. On the publishing farm server, select **Start | All Programs | Microsoft SharePoint 2010 Products | SharePoint 2010 Management Shell**.

6. In the PowerShell command prompt, type in the following command, replacing the correlation ID with the one from your screen.

```
Get-SPLogEvent | ?{$_.Correlation -eq
"xxxxxxxx-xxxx-xxxx-xxxx-xxxxxxxxxxxx"}
```

It should produce a message from the log file that reads:

There are no instances of the Web Analytics Service Application started on any server in this farm. Ensure that at least one instance is started on an application server in the farm using the Services on Server page in Central Administration.

How it works...

The PowerShell command, Get-SPLogEvent, does the job of retrieving all events in the log files. The | character sends the output of Get-SPLogEvent to the next command. The ? is the "where" command. The curly braces is the "where" condition. The $_ notation is used to represent the object being sent across the pipeline. Finally, the -eq option represents the "equal to" condition.

As a whole, this statement does a search job in the log files for a particular correlation ID, and produces the information associated with the request.

A request is traced through its lifetime. The correlation ID collects information across multiple servers maintaining the integrity of the request. As we have seen in Chapter 2, different sites can consume information from an application server that resides in a different farm but is shared. Without the correlation ID, it would be very difficult and cumbersome to trace an error.

When an error occurs, the correlation ID will have the same reference across all of the servers. This applies to WFE, application, web services, and any other components that are consumed.

There's more...

There are two other methods for looking up a correlation ID other than PowerShell. They are:

▶ Using Excel (or notepad): Log on to the Web Front End server that generated the error and navigate to the location of the ULS logs. Open the log file in Excel and utilize the find and innate filtering capabilities of Excel to find the correlation ID.

▶ Utilizing the logging database: You can execute the Accessing the *SharePoint 2010 logging database* recipe and then look for the correlation ID.

More info

On Microsoft's site, there is a free ULS viewer that can be utilized. This is not supported by Microsoft. It allows users to open a ULS log file and display its contents in a readable manner. It contains filtering, sorting, and many other functions that make the data readable. The ULS viewer can be found here: `http://code.msdn.microsoft.com/ulsviewer`.

See also

▸ *Accessing the SharePoint 2010 logging database*

Enabling the Developer Dashboard

The Developer Dashboard is not just for developers who write code. It is an important tool in the arsenal of the SharePoint Administrator.

Tools such as Microsoft's Visual Round Trip Analyzer are used to determine why a page is performing poorly. The downside of tools such as this is that they interrogate the page from the outside and so information such as database queries cannot be seen. We would have to use another tool such as SQL Profiler to see this information.

The Developer Dashboard brings this functionality natively to SharePoint 2010. It provides information, such as how a page is built, how it is performing, what database queries are being run and for how long, at the bottom of a page in report form. Administrators can use this information to pinpoint what is happening on a page.

In this recipe, we will enable the Developer Dashboard and view the report at the bottom of the page. This is done through PowerShell and can be scripted in the SharePoint environment.

Getting ready

In order to run PowerShell commands, you must be a member of the `SharePoint_Shell_Access` database role on the configuration database. You also must be a member of the `WSS_ADMIN_WPG` local group.

How to do it...

1. On the publishing farm server, select **Start | All Programs | Microsoft SharePoint 2010 Products | SharePoint 2010 Management Shell**.

2. In the PowerShell command prompt, type in the following command:

    ```
    $db = [Microsoft.SharePoint.Administration.
    SPWebService]::ContentService.DeveloperDashboardSettings;
    $db.DisplayLevel = 'On'; $db.RequiredPermissions ='EmptyMask';
    $db.TraceEnabled = $true; $db.Update()
    ```

3. Open a team site. You should see a screenshot similar to the following at the bottom of the page:

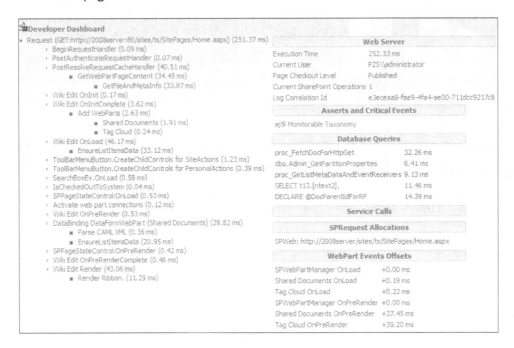

How it works...

The Developer Dashboard is a farm-wide setting. When you turn it on, the dashboard appears on page load at the bottom of the page.

The first line creates a reference to the necessary web service.

The `RequiredPermissions` parameter specifies who can see the Developer Dashboard.

Setting the trace level to `true` creates a new link called **Show or hide additional tracing information...**at the bottom of the Developer Dashboard.

There's more...

By default the Developer Dashboard is disabled.

There are three modes that can be set:

- **On**
- **Off**
- **OnDemand**

When the **OnDemand** mode is specified, a button appears in the upper right-hand corner of the page as shown here:

When clicked, the Developer Dashboard is shown, and when clicked again, it disappears.

This gives adminstrators the flexibility of enabling the Developer Dashboard without the need to make it visible always.

More info

The Developer Dashboard is available only with Windows authentication and is not available with SQL authentication.

6
Search

In this chapter, we will cover:

- ▶ Setting up Search Service
- ▶ Managing Search Service
- ▶ Scaling out the Search Service, which includes:
  - ❑ Adding a query component
  - ❑ Adding a property database
  - ❑ Adding a crawl database
- ▶ Adding a host distribution rule
- ▶ Viewing Search query/crawl reports
- ▶ Customizing the refinement menu

Introduction

The Search Service is part of the SharePoint 2010 services infrastructure. It is one of the service applications that can be shared by multiple farms. The advantage of this type of architecture is that farms do not have to configure their own search; they can subscribe to this service and can be managed at the enterprise level.

Search has been a component of SharePoint since its beginning and has evolved over time into a mature and complex product.

There are several editions of Search that an administrator should be aware of:

- ▶ **Search Server Express 2010**: This is a free product that enables users to find their content. It can search 10 million items in a fraction of a second, has the refinement panel, and contains connectors for federation and Windows file shares.

▶ **SharePoint Search Server 2010**: Bundled with Standard and Enterprise editions of SharePoint 2010, this component provides the search service for people and expertise, is integrated with My Site, and contains a phonetic/nickname search. It can search 100 million items in a subsecond.

▶ **Fast Search Server 2010**: Purchased separately for SharePoint, this edition includes thumbnail results, previews of PowerPoint presentations, and the ability to create metadata from content.

The second area of concern for the administrator is scalability. There are three components to search—a crawler, a property database, and a query server. Each component that comprises the search infrastructure can be scaled:

▶ **Crawler (Indexer)**: This component is responsible for processing content that people can later search for. The crawler generates the index files and updates the property databases.

▶ **Property Database**: This stores the metadata identified during the crawling process.

▶ **Query Server**: This component is responsible for handling the searches submitted by the site visitors. It uses the index files and property databases populated by the crawler component.

There is also an Administration database, where the crawl rules and configurations are located.

This chapter contains recipes that evolve from how to configure and scale search, to managing search, and finally addressing the usability of the search results.

Setting up Search Service

As Search Service is a part of the SharePoint 2010 services infrastructure, the setup is similar to other services. We have already gone through the setup of other services such as Excel, PerformancePoint, and the managed metadata service.

In this recipe, we will set up an instance of search through Central Administration.

Getting ready

You must have farm-level administrative permissions to the Central Administration site. Set up an Active directory account, `sa_search`. This account will be utilized to manage the Search Service.

How to do it...

1. Open the Central Administration site and click **Application Management**.

2. The third section is **Service Applications**. Under this section, click **Manages service applications**.

3. On the ribbon, click **New** and **Search Service Application**.

4. The following screenshot appears. Fill in the details.

- ❏ **Name**: This is the name for the Search Service application.

- ❏ **FAST Service Application**: Choose **None** as this book does not cover Fast Search. If you wish to read more about Fast Search, refer to the following link: `http://sharepoint.microsoft.com/en-us/product/capabilities/search/Pages/Fast-Search.aspx`.

- ❏ **Search Service Account**: Use the account that was created as a requirement of this recipe.

- ❏ **Application Pool for Search Admin Web Service**: Create a new application pool and assign the same security account that was used in the Search Service.

- ❏ **Application Pool for Search Query and Site Setting Web Service**: Utilize the same application pool used for the Search Admin Web Service.

5. Click **OK**.

How it works...

The result of this recipe creates the Search Service application and proxy. Physically, three databases are created, prefaced by the name given in step 4:

- ▶ Crawl Database
- ▶ Search Database
- ▶ Property Store Database

Additionally, a Search Administration Web Service Application is created and can be found under the **Service Applications** tab.

The application is hosted and configured on the Central Administration website.

The recipes following this one will show how to scale out the databases and move them to their own servers.

There's more...

Using PowerShell, the administrator can determine all the Search Service applications on the farm, with the help of the following command:

```
Get-SPEnterpriseSearchServiceApplication
```

See also

- ▶ *Chapter 2*, *Service Applications*. This shows how other service applications are created.

Managing Search Service

Setting up the Search Service application may be a one time job, but managing the search is not. Getting good search results to the community is the job of a vigilant administrator. As we have seen in previous recipes, the Search Administrator does not have to be the same person as the Farm Administrator.

Obtaining good search results requires monitoring trends and ensuring that content is being crawled in a timely manner. Using this information, the administrator can make appropriate decisions on how to improve performance.

This recipe introduces us to the Search Administration screen, which is used to manage the Search Service.

Getting ready

There are two ways to manage the search service:

- ▶ You can have farm-level administrative permissions to the Central Administration site
- ▶ You can be assigned as an administrator of the Search Service application

How to do it...

1. Open the Central Administration site and click **Application Management**.

2. The third section is **Service Applications**. Under this section, click **Manage service applications**.

3. Find the **Search Service Application** option and click on it (this is the name SharePoint assigns by default if not modified when creating the Search Service). The ribbon will light up. Click **Manage**.

4. The following form appears:

5. Click on the domain/username adjacent to the **Default Content Access Account** option.

6. A pop-up form titled **Default Content Access Account** appears. Put in the account that was set up for the previous recipe. Then type in the password. Click **OK**.

7. Click on the e-mail address adjacent to the **Contact e-mail address** option. Change this to the appropriate e-mail for your organization. Click **OK**.

The changes for both items should be reflected in the Search Administration screen.

How it works...

SharePoint 2010 has an extensive Search Administration screen as shown. It is broken down into four sections.

▶ The first section is the **Administration** navigation. This is the left-hand panel, where the quick launch is typically located in SharePoint. It contains four subgroups comprising of Administration, Crawling, Queries and Results, and Reports. Other recipes will address these areas.

▶ The second section is the **System Status**. This is where the performance of the crawls and queries are documented. We changed the e-mail and content account. It is important to always keep in mind the least privileged accounts. In step 6, we used the same account as the Search Service. Based on the security rules of your organization, it is a best practice to set up a different account and use it here.

The default content access account is the crawl account. Having too much access may result in the account crawling information that should not show up in the index.

▶ The third section is the **Crawl History results**. This is a summary of current and past crawls. It also shows the length of time a crawl takes, the type of crawl (Full, Incremental), and whether the crawl succeeded or failed.

▶ The last section is the **Search Application Topology**. This is where administrators can scale out a search. It shows the components of a search implemented by the server. Changing the server will show the associated components. The components shown are the following: **Administration**, **Crawl**, **Databases**, and **Index Partition**.

There's more...

The changes made in this recipe were done through the user interface. Using PowerShell is another way to make changes to Search Administration. `SPEnterprisesearchserviceapplication` is the cmdlet used to make changes to the Search Server application.

PowerShell: New Content Account

```
Set-SPEnterprisesearchserviceapplication -identity
<SearchServiceApplication>-DefaultContentAccessAccountName <accountname>
-DefaultContentAccessAccountPassword <password>
```

Scaling out Search—adding a query component

The SharePoint 2010 query server accepts the query from an end user from the web front-end. It then reads the index file and servers the result back.

The index file is partitioned. As query servers are added, the partition is broken into multiple parts so that no single query server holds the entire index. The following screenshot is from the Managing Search Topology page:

It illustrates how the index partition and query server are tied to one another. The index partition is sent to the query server by the crawl component. As can be seen from the preceding screenshot, each partition must have an associated query server.

It enhances the performance of the topology. There is no longer one large index file that must be traversed every time a query is sent.

Getting ready

You must have farm-level administrative permissions to the Central Administration site. There must also be another server on which to host the query server.

How to do it...

1. Open the Central Administration site and click **Application Management**.
2. The third section is **Service Applications**. Under this section, click **Manage service applications**.
3. Find the **Search Service Application** option and click on it (this is the name SharePoint assigns by default if not modified when creating the Search Service). The ribbon will light up. Click **Manage**.

4. Under the **Search Application Topology** section, there is a button called **Modify**; click on that button.

5. The **Search Service Topology** page appears. Click the drop-down list named **New** and then choose the **Index Partition and Query Component** option.

6. The following pop-up screen appears:

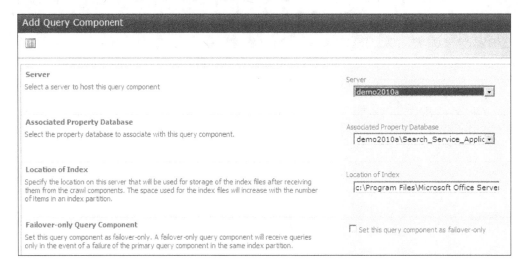

Perform the following actions:

7. Choose a server from the drop-down list.

8. Choose the property database with which it will be associated, from the **Associated Property Database** drop-down list.

9. Indicate the **Location of Index**.

10. Do not check the box associated with the **Failover-only Query Component** option.

11. Click **OK**.

12. The **Search Service Topology Application** page will again be shown. To commit the changes you have done on the previous pop-up screen, click on the **Apply Topology Changes** button.

How it works...

Creating a new query component is done through the administration page, which shows the farm's search topology. This topology can be viewed either by server or by component, using the **View** dropdown on the right-hand side of the screen. See the following screenshot:

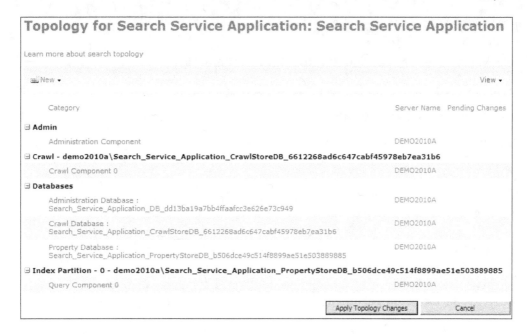

The query component returns the search results. A query server is where a query component has been created. The query component contains only part of an index partition. If there is only one query server, it would contain the whole partition.

An index partition can be spread across two or more query servers. The purpose is to reduce the size of the index on a particular query server, which translates to better performance.

Index partitions are roughly equal in size, which lends itself to the low query latency. SharePoint achieves this with the help of internal distribution by `Document ID`. Every item is internally given a `Document ID`, which is a unique identification marker.

It is important to note that an index partition is associated with a property database as we saw in the recipe.

Index partitions are not configured by users. Administrators don't know which item is sitting on which query server. Again, there is no single index (unless there is one query server).

After clicking **Apply Topology Changes**, some time may elapse before the update process is performed, as a timer job is used to perform the update.

There's more...

A new query server and partition can be added via PowerShell.

Using PowerShell, a new query can be added to the topology.

`New-SPEnterpriseSearchQueryTopology`

Using PowerShell, we can also add a new query component.

`New-SPEnterpriseSearchQueryComponent`

To see examples of these commands, type in `get-help <command> -examples` in the PowerShell management shell.

More info

A query component can be deleted from an index partition by utilizing the search topology screen we have seen above. By hovering over the item for the **Query Component**, a menu appears in the drop-down list as shown in the following screenshot. Click **Delete**.

See also

- ▶ *Adding a property database*
- ▶ *Adding a crawl database*

Scaling out Search—adding a property database

As we saw in the previous recipe, the index partition is associated with a property database. As your site grows and the items in the index grow, metadata needs become a possible bottleneck.

This information is stored in the property database. If users are performing many metadata searches, then more property databases (either on the same or separate SQL Servers) may need to be added to relieve this congestion. This recipe shows how to achieve this.

Getting ready

You must have farm-level administrative permissions to the Central Administration site.

How to do it...

1. Open the Central Administration and click **Application Management**.

2. The third section is **Service Applications**. Under this section, click **Manage service applications**.

3. Find the **Search Service Application** option and click on it (this is the name SharePoint assigns by default if not modified when creating the Search Service). The ribbon will light up. Click **Manage**.

4. Under the **Search Application Topology** section, there is a button called **Modify**; click this button.

5. The **Search Service Topology** page appears. Click the drop-down list named **New** and select **Property Database**.

6. The following pop up appears:

Perform the following actions:

7. Enter the name of a database server.

8. Enter a name for the property database in the **Database Name** textbox.

9. Select the **Windows authentication** option under **Database authentication**.

10. If you have the name of a Failover Server, enter it in the appropriate textbox. Click **OK**.

11. The **Search Service Topology Application** page will appear again. To commit the changes you have done on the screen, click on the **Apply Topology Changes** button.

How it works...

When the above recipe is executed, a new property database is created. This can be viewed via SQL Management Studio.

In order to put it to use, this property database must be assigned to a query component (as seen in the preceding recipe).

There's more...

A new property database can be created and added via PowerShell.

Use the following command to add a new property database:

```
New-SPEnterpriseSearchPropertyDatabase
```

To see examples of the above command, type `get-help <command> -examples` in the PowerShell management shell.

See also

► *Adding a query component*

Scaling out Search—adding a crawl database

The final component that can be scaled out with regards to search is crawler. In the topology search application page, it is broken into two items:

► Crawl Database

► Crawl Component

The Crawl Server comprises of the crawl component that is associated with a crawl database. Each crawl database has one or more crawl components (crawlers) to index its content. It is typically scaled out for redundancy purposes or to increase the speed of the crawl.

The crawler crawls the content sources and creates the index partition(s). Then it sends the created partition(s) to the query server(s). It does not hold the index partition. It writes details about the crawl into the crawl database. It is stateless in that it does not retain information itself.

Getting ready

You must have farm-level administrative permissions to the Central Administration site.

How to do it...

1. Open the Central Administration site and click **Application Management**.

2. The third section is **Service Applications**. Under this section, click **Manage service applications**.

3. Find the **Search Service Application** option and click on it (this is the name SharePoint assigns by default if not modified when creating the Search Service). The ribbon will light up. Click **Manage**.

4. Under the **Search Application Topology** section, there is a button called **Modify**; click this button.

5. The **Search Service Topology** page appears. Click the drop-down list named **New** and select **Crawl Database.**

6. The pop-up screen that appears is almost exactly like the property database pop up seen in the preceding recipe.

   Fill in the following elements:

7. Enter the name of a database server.

8. Enter a name for the crawl database.

9. Select the **Windows authentication** option under **Database authentication** section.

10. If you have the name of a Failover Server, enter it in the appropriate textbox.

11. There is one more item in the pop-up that needs to be addressed. As shown in the next screen, do not check the **Dedicate this crawl...** box. It will be addressed in the *Adding a host distribution rule* recipe.

Dedicated Database	
Select this setting to indicate that this crawl store should be dedicated to hosts as specified in Host Distribution Rules. It is not possible to set a crawl store as dedicated once a crawl store has been created.	☐ Dedicate this crawl store to hosts as specified in Host Distribution Rules

   Click **OK**.

12. The **Search Service Topology Application** page will be shown again. To commit the changes you have done in the previous screen, click the **Apply Topology Changes** button.

13. Click the drop-down list named **New** and select **Crawl Component**.

14. The following pop-up screen appears:

Server	Server
Select a server to host this crawl component.	demo2010a
Associated Crawl Database	Associated Crawl Database
Select the crawl database to associate with this crawl component.	demo2010a\Search_Service_Applic
Temporary Location of Index	Temporary Location of Index
Specify the location on this server that will be used for creating the index files before propagating them to the query components. The space required in this directory will be relatively small and constant, independent of the total number of items crawled.	c:\Program Files\Microsoft Office Server

Perform the following steps:

15. Choose a server from the drop-down list, on which to host the crawl component.

16. Choose the associated crawl database from the drop-down list.

17. Specify a location for the index by entering the value in the **Temporary Location of Index** textbox.

Click **OK**.

18. The **Search Service Topology Application** page will again be shown. To commit the changes you have done on the screen, click the **Apply Topology Changes** button.

How it works...

The creation of the crawl database is similar to the property database. A new database is added to the farm and can be seen physically via SQL Management Studio.

The only additional item is using host distribution rules, which will be covered in the *Adding a host distribution rule* recipe.

The crawl component, which is created after the database, creates a temporary index that gets stored on the Crawl Server. This index is eventually propagated and overwritten.

The crawl content and the data such as the location of the content source are saved in the crawl database. It is the crawler's job to propagate partition-indexed data to the query servers.

The crawler is truly a stateless object.

There's more...

Everything done using the UI can be scripted via PowerShell in order to automate the procedure.

Use the following command to create a new crawl database:

```
New-SPEnterpriseSearchCrawlDatabase
```

Use the following command to create a new crawl component:

```
New-SPEnterpriseSearchCrawlComponent
```

To see examples of these commands, type `get-help <command> -examples` in the PowerShell management shell.

More info

A crawl topology can contain multiple crawl components. By mapping multiple crawl components to a single crawl database, performance will increase and fault tolerance is achieved.

If one of the crawl components crashes, the remaining crawl components step in and perform the indexing.

If the crawler database server fails and you have specified a failover database server, SharePoint will automatically switch over to use it. However, this requires your SQL Servers to use synchronous mirroring. Asynchronous mirroring is not supported in this case.

See also

▸ *Adding a host distribution rule*

Adding a host distribution rule

One of the configuration items that an administrator has more control over is the ability to dedicate a host address to a specific crawl database. A crawl database contains data related to the location of content sources and crawl schedules. It may be a benefit to the user base that certain content is indexed more frequently in order to be fresher.

This is done through host distribution rules. A database can be dedicated to a server (or host).

In this recipe, we will create a host distribution rule.

Getting ready

You must have farm-level administrative permissions to the Central Administration site.

There must be at least two crawl databases. Create the second crawl database as shown in the previous recipe, except checking of the box under **Dedicate Database**.

How to do it...

1. Open Central Administration and click **Application Management**.

2. The third section is **Service Applications**. Under this section, click **Manage service applications**.

3. Find the **Search Service Application** option and click on it (this is the name SharePoint assigns by default if not modified when creating the Search Service). The ribbon will light up. Click **Manage**.

4. On the left-hand navigation, under the section marked **Crawling**, click **Host Distribution Rules**.

5. At the top of the displayed page, you can see the **Add Distribution Rule** option; click this option.

6. The following screen appears:

- ❑ Enter the hostname that contains the content you want to index (for example, accounting.contoso.com).

- ❑ Select the crawl database that you want to make responsible for crawling the specified hostname.

    Click **OK**.

7. Click **Apply Changes**.

8. A confirmation screen appears. Click **Redistribute Now**.

How it works...

When indicating an existing host, the content is physically moved and assigned to the crawl database that was selected.

In the recipe, we set up a dedicated host name distribution rule. When a crawl database is designated to a host stored in the rules, the crawl will not allocate any new host addresses into this crawl database. This means the host (or server) is a one crawl database.

By default, servers are load-balanced across crawl databases.

The efficiency of this setup evinces itself when a particular host has millions of items to be crawled. Dedicating a crawl database for the content is efficient and reduces disk latency.

There's more...

Host distribution rules can be used to redistribute host addresses that have already been indexed. By redistributed we mean adding another crawl database. By following the recipe above, the host addresses will be redistributed and the host distribution rule can then be deleted.

See also

 ▶ *Adding a crawl database*

Viewing Search Query/Crawl Reports

The preceding recipes have shown the scalability of the SharePoint Search infrastructure. Search topology is robust and flexible. As the needs of the organization grow, Search can scale.

The question becomes a matter of when, not if, Search must be scaled. It is also a question of where (which components) to scale Search.

The answers to these questions are found in the set of reports that ship with SharePoint 2010. There are two basic types of search administration reports:

 ▶ **Reports that address query processing**. These reports show the latency of the queries.
 ▶ **Reports that show information about the crawler**. These reports show processing in the queue, per component, per content source, and per type.

In this recipe, we will show how to view and find them.

Getting ready

You must have farm-level administrative permissions to the Central Administration site.

Your farm must be set up to crawl content and must have completed a full crawl. In addition, the site must have been in use by users in order to collect information on queries.

How to do it...

1. Open Central Administration and click **Monitoring**.

2. The third section is **Reporting**. Under this section, click **View administrative reports**.

3. Click on the folder named `Search administrative reports`.

4. Click on the report titled **Crawl Rate Per Content Source**.

5. The information is presented in the form of the graphical view on top and a grid below:

Search Service Application	Content Source	Crawl Start	Crawl Duration (min)	Crawl rate (items per minute)
Enterprise Search Service Application	Local SharePoint sites	12/7/2010 7:56:00 AM	1	7
Enterprise Search Service Application	Anchor Crawl	12/7/2010 7:58:00 AM	1	2
Enterprise Search Service Application	Local SharePoint sites	12/8/2010 7:56:00 AM	0	14
Enterprise Search Service Application	Anchor Crawl	12/8/2010 7:58:00 AM	0	2
Enterprise Search Service Application	Local SharePoint sites	12/9/2010 7:56:00 AM	0	17
Enterprise Search Service Application	Anchor Crawl	12/9/2010 7:57:00 AM	1	2

How it works...

The reports are `.aspx` pages saved in a document library. The information is taken from the usage logging database. These reports can be edited or created in SharePoint Designer.

There's more...

There are filters along the top of the reports, in order to look at the data in a more granular fashion. The filters for the above report are:

- **Application**: Listing of the Search Service applications. These are listed with radio buttons in order to choose one.

- **Content Sources** (some of the reports): Listing of all the content sources that are set up in the scope, for example, items such as websites or information in file shares. In addition, it lists all of the content sources by search application.

- **Start Date**: Reports the start date of the report.

- **End Date**: Reports the end date of the report.

When finished choosing the filters, there is an **Apply Filters** button on the right ready to be clicked.

Application	Content Sources	Start Date			End Date			Apply Filters
Search Service Application	Search Service Application. Lo	11/27/2010	1 PM	27	11/28/2010	1 AM	42	

Customizing the refinement menu

The SharePoint 2010 Search Center results page contains a new section called the refinement panel. This panel is located on the left portion of the screen and provides a summary of search results which, when used, act as filters on the returned data.

Out of the box, there are three main categories:

- ▶ Site
- ▶ Author
- ▶ Date

New custom refinement categories can be configured, these are based on managed properties. Managed properties are the metadata stored with items in SharePoint. There are many more properties than the three that are shown out of the box.

This recipe consists of two parts:

- ▶ Adding a managed property, which takes place in the Central Administration.
- ▶ Modifying the refinement menu to include a new category based on the managed property, which will be done at the site level.

Getting ready

Ensure that you are a Site Collection Administrator.

In the site, you are going to modify a custom list and create a new column called `Finance`, using the property named **Single Line of Text**. Upload a couple of documents into the library and assign a value to Finance for each one. Use something as simple as 1 or 2 as the value.

Create an **Enterprise Search Center Site**. This is available with the enterprise edition. Call it **SearchCenter**.

Modify the **Search Settings** under **Site Collection Administration** (found under **Site Actions**) so that the site you are testing against points to `/SearchCenter/Pages/results.aspx`.

You must have farm-level administrative permissions to the Central Administration site.

How to do it...

Part 1: Creating Managed Property

1. Open the Central Administration site and click **Application Management**.

2. The third section is **Service Applications**. Under this section, click **Manage service applications**.

3. Find the **Search Service Application** option and click on it (this is the name SharePoint assigns by default if not modified when creating the Search Service). The ribbon will light up. Click **Manage**.

4. On the left-hand navigation, under the section marked **Queries and Results**, click **Metadata Properties**.

5. Click **New Managed Property**. A new form appears.

6. In the **Name** textbox, type **Finance**.

7. Under **Mappings to crawled properties**, click **Add Mapping**.

8. The following pop-up screen appears:

9. In the **Select a category** listbox, select **SharePoint**.

10. Navigate to the Finance property.

    Click **OK**.

11. On the **New Managed Property** page, check the box for **Use in Scopes**. Click **OK**.

12. Initiate a full crawl on the **Local SharePoint sites** (under **Content Sources**).

Part 2: Creating Custom Refiner

1. Navigate to the Search Center page, for example, `servername/SearchCenter/Pages/results.aspx`.

2. Perform a search. Click **Site Actions, Edit Page**.

3. In the web part marked **Refinement Panel**, select **Edit Web Part** from the drop-down list.

4. Under the section **Refinement**, there is the **Filter Category Definition**. Click the **...** box to the right of this.

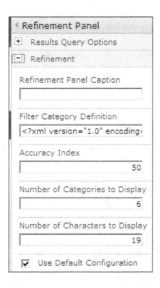

5. You are presented with a text editor of the contents. Select all of the text (*Ctrl+A*) and copy and paste the contents into Notepad.

6. Run a search query on `Author`. Copy the author's category tag. It will contain the following:

```
<Category     Title="Author"     Description="Use this
filter to restrict results authored by a specific
author"    Type="Microsoft.Office.Server.Search.WebControls.
ManagedPropertyFilterGenerator"     MetadataThreshold="5"
NumberOfFiltersToDisplay="4"     MaxNumberOfFilters="20"
SortBy="Frequency"     SortByForMoreFilters="Name"
SortDirection="Descending"     SortDirectionForMoreFilters="A
scending"    ShowMoreLink="True"     MappedProperty="Author"
MoreLinkText="show more"     LessLinkText="show fewer"     />
```

7. Paste the copied tag right after the end of the original `Author` tag.

8. Make the following changes:

   a. Change the `Title` to `Finance`.

   b. Change the `MetadataThreshold` to `1`.

   c. Change `MappedProperty` to `Finance`.

9. Copy and paste the complete text from the Notepad (where we copied the text to in step 5) into the text editor. Click **OK**.

10. Ensure the **Use Default Configuration** option is unchecked.

11. Click **Apply** and then **OK** on the **Web part properties** dialog.

12. Check in and publish page.

13. Perform a search by your name. Doing this makes the assumption that there are documents with your name in them, about you, or created by you.

How it works...

The refiner panel is a web part on the Search results page that contains properties to completely configure the way it looks and behaves. In this recipe, we utilized the Refinement XML configuration to add a new category.

Part 1 of our recipe creates the managed property. A prerequisite of this recipe was to create a column that we could consume. Once this was done and the content was crawled, the property becomes available to define as a managed property. This part is done by a Search Administrator or the Farm Administrator.

Part 2 of our recipe took that property and mapped it to a category of our creation. We performed this in step 15. This is done at the site level. The end result is a panel that looks like the following screenshot:

```
Site
Any Site
2008server/sites/ts
2008server/ATM

Author
Any Author
pzs\administrator
AutoBVT

Finance
Any Finance
Loan

Modified Date
Any Modified Date
Past 24 Hours
Past Six Months

Tags
Any Tags
EBITDA
sample
```

There's more...

The property **Metadata Threshold** is critical to have the category show up, as you expected, in the refinement panel. The value of this property will be compared against the count of metadata matches. If the number of matches is higher than the value, the refiner category will show.

This gives you control over how many and what refiners are shown in the panel. This can be used to prevent the panel from becoming too crowded.

More info

In the preceding screenshot, there is a section called Tags. When doing a search for information, the returned results may be categorized by information found in the Managed Metadata Term Store.

That is what we see here. EBITDA was added into the Term Store back in *Chapter 4, Site Administration*, and is now being flagged as a filter in the result set.

7
Security Administration: Users and Groups

In this chapter, we will cover:

- ▶ Adding a user via PowerShell
- ▶ Delegating PowerShell permissions
- ▶ Checking effective permission user interface
- ▶ Setting Lockdown Mode for publishing sites
- ▶ Configuring Site Collection audit settings
- ▶ Accessing security policy reports

Introduction

Security of the SharePoint Farm is critical to the health and governance of the SharePoint implementation. It is important to understand the varied ways in which SharePoint can be secured.

The term **secured** in this chapter pertains to what information and permissions users need in order to be effective. As an administrator, it is critical to be able to determine who did what and when.

Successful server hardening depends on planning an appropriate server topology and logical architecture. This architecture is then implemented into the physical navigation and creation of libraries and lists. This should provide the appropriate isolation of data.

SharePoint groups can then be created, which follows the physical topology of the site.

Adverse issues with security will not just affect the ability for users to access content, but will also allow these items to be visible in people's searches. In real world terms, if employment data is saved in SharePoint, this information may be available to every person in the organization.

Giving users the appropriate access to the information to do their jobs is addressed in the first recipe. Setting audit controls and being able to report on those controls will be addressed in the last two recipes.

Adding a user via PowerShell

When SharePoint is initially set up, many users may need to be added to SharePoint groups for a new site. The quickest and most efficient way to accomplish this is through PowerShell and scripting.

The following recipe shows how to add a user to a SharePoint group via PowerShell.

Getting ready

The user must have access to one of the servers running PowerShell 2.0 and be a member of the `WSS_ADMIN_WPG` on the local computer. You must also be a member of the `SharePoint_Shell_Access` role on the configuration database (SQL Role).

There must be an existing site, a SharePoint group called `TestAddUser`, and a user named `jdoe` set up in the active directory.

How to do it...

1. Click on the **Start** button on the web front end.

2. Under **All Programs**, navigate to the `Microsoft SharePoint 2010 Products` folder.

3. Right-click on the **SharePoint 2010 Management Shell** option and click **Run as Administrator**. The PowerShell console will appear.

4. Type the following command into the console window, replacing the parameter values with ones that are relevant to your environment:

   ```
   New-spuser -web http://sitename -useralias "PZSjdoe" -group
   "TestAddUser"
   ```

5. The result of the operation is shown here:

```
UserLogin                 DisplayName
---------                 -----------
PZS\jdoe                  John Doe
```

How it works...

Using PowerShell with SharePoint, the `Microsoft.SharePoint.PowerShell` snapin must be added using the `Add-PSSnapin` cmdlet. This is done automatically when you use the SharePoint 2010 Management Shell.

PowerShell is integrated with the .NET framework. SharePoint exposes its management capability to PowerShell. The SharePoint object model is also available via PowerShell. The power of PowerShell is the ability to script commands together. These commands are referred to as cmdlets.

Cmdlets follow a `<verb>` `<noun>` naming pattern.

There's more...

The following PowerShell commands provide users with management functionality:

- `Get-SPUser`: Returns a user after matching the record with the provided criteria. The common criteria are user identity and website where they are a user.
- `Remove-SPUser`: Deletes a user from a site.
- `Move-SPUser`: Moves a user account into the provided site.
- `Set-SPUser`: Configuration of user properties.

More info

You can combine several cmdlets together to create a script, saving the file with a `.ps1` extension. The script could reference a file containing a list of active directory user accounts. This will allow you to do a batch upload of the users to the designated sites and groups.

Delegating PowerShell permissions

One of the many promises SharePoint 2010 delivers on is the empowering of users. In other words, SharePoint 2010 allows an administrator to delegate responsibility down to the other administrative user. The concern with doing this is exposing other administrative tasks. Just because someone can manage an application, such as Search, does not mean they should be able to manage other service applications. SharePoint 2010 handles this without putting at risk the security of the other components. Farm Administrators can designate users to manage their own service application, as we have seen in Chapter 2. This is done through the management UI of each service application. Taking this management one step further, a Farm Administrator can designate a user with the ability to run PowerShell commands against their particular service(s) from their own machines.

The least privileged account model in SharePoint has been taken to another level. Users have access to manage only what you, as an administrator, have designated to them.

This recipe will show how to grant PowerShell access to a user so that they can manage their service applications.

Getting ready

You must have farm-level administrative permissions. A user must be set up in the active directory—the recipe will use the domain \jdoe. Replace domain with the appropriate value from your installation.

You will need the name of the service application database to which you are assigning rights. You can get this with the help of the following PowerShell command:

```
GetSPServiceApplication-SPServiceApplication
```

How to do it...

1. Click on the **Start** button on the web front end server.

2. Under **All Programs**, navigate to the Microsoft SharePoint 2010 Products folder.

3. Right-click on the **SharePoint 2010 Management Shell** option and click **Run as Administrator**. The PowerShell console will appear.

4. Type the following command into the console window:

   ```
   Add-SPShellAdmin –username domain\jdoe
   ```

   Press the *Enter* key.

5. Type the following into the console window, replacing the parameter values with ones relevant to your environment:

```
Add-SPShellAdmin -username domain\jdoe -database 047e05eb-2d68-
46a1-b0e0-e9ac92e99ff8
```

Press the *Enter* key again.

How it works...

The first command did the following two things:

- It added the user to the `SharePoint_Shell_Access` role in the farm configuration database. If the role was not in the database, it is created automatically. When the user is added, the role grants the users, `db_owner` as well as `securityadmin`, with the rights to the farm configuration database.
- It added the user to the `WSS_ADMIN_WPG` local security group on each server in the farm.

The second command added the parameter named `database`. We targeted a specific content database (using its GUID in this case) and the user was added to the `SharePoint_Shell_Access` role for that database. Additionally, the user is added to the role in the Central Administration content database.

There's more...

Using PowerShell, an administrator can obtain a list of names that are part of the `SharePoint_Shell_Access` role, with the help of the following command:

```
Get-SPShellAdmin
```

More info

The most effective use of PowerShell is in regards to scripting. Actions can be automated. Automation comes in the guise of writing code. Combine this statement with the type of access that is granted in this recipe—`db_owner`. This should not be granted without any thought, for example, power users should not be conferred with so much authority.

A typical power user cannot write, and should not be authorized to write code, in order to automate things such as uploading a Term Set to the managed metadata service. On top of that, a power user *should not* be granted the `db_owner` access as is shown in this recipe.

Note that PowerShell does not do security trimming. When a user is given this ability on a database, they have `db_owner` access to everything in that database.

However, the administrator of the farm may not have time to automate functions. A Farm Administrator can delegate this responsibility to the appropriate person who has the ability to write the PowerShell code. That person can be granted ownership of the service.

Anyone who has the capability must understand the code and, even more importantly, the ramifications of their script with regards to the topology of the farm. For instance, if a developer is granted db_owner access to a content database that houses several site collections, the developer now has full access to all the site collections in the content database.

Checking effective permission user interface

Once SharePoint 2010 is rolled out into an environment, it takes on a life of its own. Team sites, project sites, and other collaboration sites are created to fit the pressing business needs.

Along with each of these sites, security may be manipulated by breaking inheritance. This type of granularity breeds complexity. Sites are provisioned but not decommissioned due to the sheer number of sites. It is a common request from users to know what sites they have access to and what permissions they have on those sites. There is functionality within sites that provides such information.

The following recipe shows how to use this functionality.

Getting ready

You must be a site owner or site collection administrator.

How to do it...

1. Navigate to the desired team site.
2. Click **Site Actions** and then **Site Permissions**.
3. Click the **Check Permissions** option on the ribbon.
4. The following screen pops up:

5. Enter the name of a user or group.
6. Click **Check Now**. The resulting permission levels for that person or group are displayed as seen in the following screenshot:

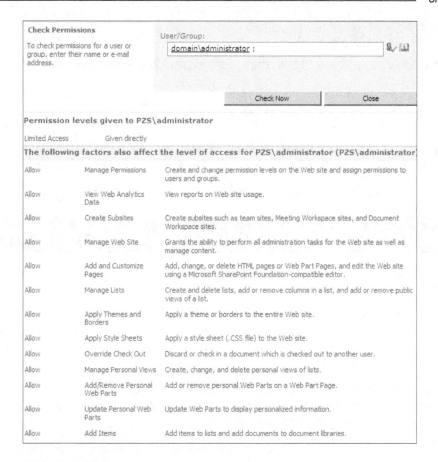

How it works...

SharePoint 2010 uses the people picker control to verify the user or group. When this is submitted, SharePoint looks through the site to determine the permission levels that this account has been assigned. Note that you will see only those permissions that the account has on the current site. Permissions that the account has to any other subsites are not shown.

The Limited Access permission is to be used with sites that have granular permissions. For instance, if a user is given access to only a library on a site, the user still needs access to the parent website and be able to use shared information such as the navigation. Limited Access provides this and cannot be customized or deleted.

There's more...

Under the ribbon, after step 2 of this recipe, we may see the following message being displayed:

> Some content on this site has unique permissions which are not controlled from this page. Show me uniquely secured content

By clicking on the **Show me uniquely secured content** link, you will be shown a pop-up window, listing any objects that have unique permissions. Comments are also listed.

This is a useful feature for managing lists that have unique permissions.

Setting Lockdown Mode for publishing sites

When implementing external facing sites, it is critical that administrators be aware of what users can do under given conditions.

A common scenario on a site is to have a blog or article page and then have a comments section below it. In the SharePoint terminology, this implies that anonymous users can write back to a list. Think about this, a viewer of your site has the ability to add an item to a list (in the form of a comment).

By default, if the root site is a blog site, anonymous users can add comments. However, if a site collection is based on the publishing portal, they will not be able to add comments or articles to a blog that lives under the site collection.

In this recipe, we will see how to manipulate the feature that will enable anonymous users to add comments to a blog or article.

Getting ready

You must have access to one of the servers running PowerShell 2.0 and be a member of the `WSS_ADMIN_WPG` on the local computer. You must also be a member of the `SharePoint_Shell_Access` role on the configuration database (SQL role).

There must be a site created, based on the publishing portal template.

How to do it...

1. Click on the **Start** button on the web front end.
2. Under **All Programs**, navigate to the `Microsoft SharePoint 2010 Products` folder.

3. Right-click on the **SharePoint 2010 Management Shell** option and click **Run as Administrator**. The PowerShell console will appear.

4. Type the following command into the console window:

```
$ldstatus = get-spfeature viewformpageslockdown
Disable-spfeature $ldstatus -url http://sitecollectionURL
```

How it works...

SharePoint 2010 has a feature called `ViewFormPagesLockdown`. This feature prevents or enables anonymous users to gain access to standard list forms and particular sections of your site. It is automatically turned on for publishing sites.

Anonymous users' rights are determined by the Limited Access permission level. Limited Access cannot be assigned to a user or group directly. If you have a subsite that you break permission on and give a user access, that user needs some type of access to the root site. This is done through Limited Access permissions.

By using PowerShell as shown in the preceding recipe, the `ViewFormPagesLockdown` feature is disabled at the site collection level. Now anonymous users can add comments to a blog or article.

There's more...

Using PowerShell, an administrator can determine if lockdown is enabled on the site, with the help of the following command:

```
Get-spfeature -site http://sitecollectionurl
```

A list of features is displayed. If `ViewFormPagesLockDown` is shown in the list, it is enabled.

Configuring Site Collection audit settings

Often in a SharePoint site, it is important to know who is doing what and when. For instance, in a publishing site, sometimes users do things they don't mean to do and it is important to audit these events.

In many cases, it is mandatory to be able to track what happens to a document—especially in the case of sensitive company information, information related to ISO certifications, or some other type of industry standard.

In this recipe, we will show how to enable the settings at a site collection level so that all actions may be tracked. These include checking in a document, checking out documents, deletes, additions, and modifications to items.

Getting ready

You must have site collection owner privileges.

How to do it...

1. Navigate to the desired team site, which is the root site collection.
2. Click on **Site Actions** and then **Site Settings**.
3. Under **Site Collection Administration**, click **Site collection audit settings**.
4. The following form will be displayed:

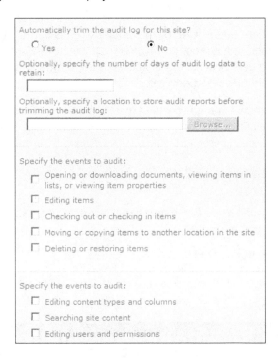

Fill the form as follows:

5. Leave the default as **No** under **Audit log trimming**.
6. Under **Specify the events to audit** (for documents and items), select all of the checkboxes.
7. Under **Specify the events to audit** (for lists, libraries, and sites), check all of the boxes.

   Click **OK**.

How it works...

The first section is for audit log trimming. When creating an audit trail in our recipe, every event is tracked and logged for every user and process. The audit log can quickly fill up the space on your drive and in your database. As an administrator, it is crucial to be aware of this.

Specifying the number of days to retain is a smart way to trim your log. If you do need it, there is an option to store the audit log before it is trimmed.

The second section pertains to documents and items. In many cases it is not necessary to select all of the options. Sometimes the site collection administrator just needs to track when documents are deleted. Again, choosing all of the options fills up the audit log quickly.

The last section pertains to site content, users, and permissions. SharePoint is now a repository where mission-critical data is held, and user permissions are paramount to passing an audit. It may be necessary to select only the checkbox, so that the auditors have the evidence they need to ensure the compliance of your organization to set rules.

Accessing security policy reports

In the previous recipe, we configured the auditing settings. We need to read this information and evaluate what is happening on our site.

The security policy reports show us what is going on in our sites. In this recipe, we will show how to run the reports.

Getting ready

You must have site collection owner privileges.

How to do it...

1. Navigate to the desired team site, which is the root site collection.
2. Click on **Site Actions** and then **Site Settings**.
3. Under **Site Collection Administration**, click **Audit log reports**.

4. Scroll to the bottom of the resulting screen. It should be similar to the following screenshot:

5. Click **Auditing settings**.

6. A form pops up with a text box where we must put a **save location** for the report. Using the **Browse** button, navigate to **Shared Documents**.

7. Click **OK**.

8. A screen will appear with a link to the generated report, click this link. The report will appear in the Excel format.

How it works...

These reports are fed by the previous recipe options. When the report is generated, it is saved to the selected location, in the Excel format, and is date and time stamped.

You can navigate to that location, select the report, and view it.

See also

▶ *Configuring Site Collection audit settings*

8
Content Management

In this chapter, we will cover:

- ▸ Configuring advanced routing (Content Organizer)
- ▸ Routing documents to another site
- ▸ Configuring content deployment
- ▸ Adding a Content Type hub
- ▸ Managing External Content Types
- ▸ Creating a Term Set
- ▸ Importing a Term Set
- ▸ In place Records Management

Introduction

Since the release of SharePoint, content management using SharePoint is one of its key tenets. Many companies implement SharePoint based on its strong document management capabilities.

As the needs of an organization grow, so does the content it has to handle and the need to manage it appropriately. File saving and sharing is easier when a company is smaller and everyone participates in the storage of documents. Exposing information to the outside world is manageable because only one or two people may be responsible for the management of information. There is little duplication of efforts or information.

As companies grow, the complexity in processes grow. This results in the increased need for storage and, as a result, things may become unmanageable. Companies go from having one or two file shares to having several. Multiple people now need to review and approve documents before they are shared. As a result, those documents and versions are propagated across the organization.

An example of this is the Request for Quote process. Several individuals need to input information into this process and, as a result, one document may be found on several local computers and in several file shares. Each document may be a different version.

IT can become a bottleneck in exposing information to the public. They may be solely responsible for the web server and putting information into web pages.

SharePoint does its job to address these pains through the implementation of its enterprise content management. This functionality must be configured to be leveraged. Also, SharePoint is built on a .NET foundation, which provides a lot of flexibility for extending SharePoint's use as a platform. Of course this may mean writing server-side code, which may be against the governance policies of an organization.

The recipes presented in this chapter cover the different facets of content management from an administrator's perspective.

Content types, which provide a construct to define and structure our metadata in SharePoint, have an additional role to play in SharePoint 2010. Two new functionalities are covered in this chapter—the Content Type hub and External Content Type. The former allows for the sharing of content types across site collections, whereas the latter provides functionality to define a structure that is part of an external business system (that is CRM). In addition, several new content types, such as the document set and several new business intelligence content types, have been added.

Term Sets are new and allow an organization to have a common terminology. When tagging items and documents in SharePoint, all of the workers use the same terminology.

Routing and Records Management allows organizations to catalog information and manage the whereabouts and lifetime of that data.

Finally, using a combination of the recipes shown will allow the SharePoint Administrator to empower end users to focus on their content management issues, minimizing the concern of Records Management.

Configuring advanced routing (Content Organizer)

SharePoint 2010 contains the capability to route documents to folders and libraries. SharePoint can even route documents between site collections, as long as the Content Organizer is configured in source and destination. The Content Organizer is the function that manages these documents.

Folders within libraries are part of this feature, which gives added flexibility to users who are comfortable with this type of organization. Routing is very useful when managing limits within document libraries, routing items such as proposals and RFPs, and using managed metadata to determine where documents should reside.

Routing is determined via predefined rules. In this recipe, we will configure the Content Organizer, set up a rule, and route a document.

Getting ready

You must have a site set up and should be the owner of that site.

How to do it...

1. Open up the SharePoint website.

2. Click **Site Actions**, then **Site Settings**.

3. Under the **Site Actions** section, click **Manage site features**.

4. The first feature listed is the **Content Organizer**. Click on the **Activate** button to the right of the feature.

5. Click **Site Settings**. Two new menu items have been added to the Site Administration section. Refer to the next screenshot:

Content Organizer Settings
Content Organizer Rules

6. Click **Content Organizer Rules**.

7. Click the **Add new item** link.

8. The following pop-up screen appears:

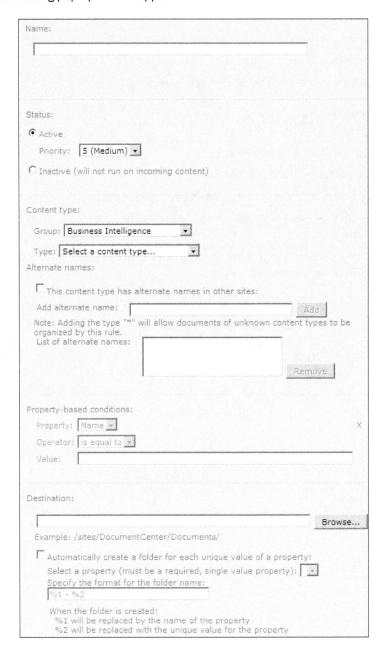

Fill in the fields as follows:

- **Name**: Enter **CashFlow** in the textbox.
- **Status**: Leave this as the default value, that is, **Active**.
- **Content type Group**: Select **Document Content Types** from the drop-down list.
- **Content Type**: Select **Document** from the drop-down list.
- **Property**: Select **Managed Keywords** from the drop-down list.
- **Operator**: **is equal to** (which is selected by default).
- **Value**: Enter **EBITDA** in the textbox.
- **Destination**: Click **Browse** and navigate to Shared Documents.

Click **OK**.

9. Click **Drop Off Library** and then **Add new document**.

10. Click the **Browse** button. Choose a document to upload and click **OK**.

11. Fill in the form as follows:

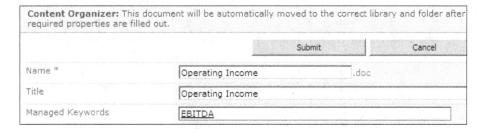

12. Click **Submit**. A message appears notifying you of the document's final location.

How it works...

Routing is configured at the site level and not at the site collection level. Activating the feature not only creates the two menu items as outlined in step 5, but also creates a document library called Drop Off Library. All uploads are sent to this library. This is a document library that has the standard features such as workflow, approvals, check in/check out, alerts, and permissions.

Rules are based on content type and can contain multiple conditions. In the example, we based the rule on Managed Metadata (EBITDA).

If the uploaded document did not meet the rule's condition, then the document would remain in the Drop Off Library. E-mails would be generated to the rule managers (if the box to send e-mails was checked).

By default, the Drop Off Library option manages content types. The result of this is that when a rule is created for a content type that is not native to the Drop Off Library, it will be added dynamically.

There's more...

The second menu item added under **Site Settings** is **Content Organizer Settings**. This is where the configuration settings for the Content Organizer are found. The following are the options:

- ▶ **Redirect Users to the Drop Off Library**: Checking this box redirects users to the Drop Off Library when they try and upload content in the site. This means that no matter what library you try and upload content to, you will be redirected to the Drop Off Library pop-up window shown in step 11. After entering the metadata and submitting the document, it is routed as per the routing rules.

  If this box is not enabled, only uploading to the Drop Off Library will enable a document to be routed as per the rules.

- ▶ **Sending to Another Site**: When checking this box, a document can be routed, as per the rules, to another site that has the Content Organizer feature activated. It provides a drop-down list of the targeted destinations. This is covered in the next recipe.

- ▶ **Folder Partitioning**: When checking this box, a subfolder is dynamically created after the maximum number of items (specified in the option) in the store is reached. The new item is routed to the new folder and the name of the folder is controlled by the second parameter. **%1**, the default setting, is substituted with the date/time stamp. The number of items and folder names is controlled by the owner of the site.

- ▶ **Duplicate Submissions**: When a document has the same name as a document already in the destination library, we need to choose one of the two options. If versioning is turned on, a new version of the document is added. The other option appends unique characters to the end of the file.

- ▶ **Preserving Context**: The original audit logs and properties for a document are kept with it after it is routed.

- ▶ **Rule Managers**: This is a management configuration. Owners are not the only people who can create rules and manage the Drop Off Library. There are two checkbox options, where both the rules are related to receiving e-mails. Enabling the first checkbox will cause the rule managers to receive an e-mail when an item does not match a rule. The second check box has the effect of sending e-mails to the rule managers when items are left in the Drop Off Library.

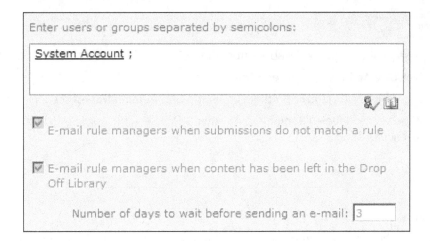

- **Submission Points**: A URL to the web service is presented. This option is useful when setting up other sites and workflows for routing.

Routing documents to another site

This recipe builds upon the previous recipe that showed how to route documents between document libraries in a site.

Using Content Organizer, it is possible to route documents to different sites. There are many uses for this type of functionality. For instance, proposals can be uploaded to a common site but routed to an appropriate site based on its metadata properties.

This gives an out of the box power to SharePoint, which is beneficial to users. It also helps manage the size of document libraries through intelligent routing. No longer does an organization need to keep all documents in one place and then implement an archiving solution when the library grows too large.

This recipe shows how to implement the aforementioned functionality.

Getting ready

You must have farm-level administrative permissions to the Central Administration site.

You must have two sites set up and you should be the owner of these sites.

How to do it...

1. Open up the SharePoint website from the last recipe. It contains the Drop Off Library.

2. Click **Site Actions**, then **Site Settings**.

3. Click **Content Organizer Settings** under the **Site Administration** section.

4. In the section labeled **Sending to Another Site**, check the box shown in the next screenshot:

5. Click **OK**.

6. Open the second SharePoint website B that was created as part of the requirements.

7. Click **Site Actions**, then **Site Settings**.

8. Under the **Site Actions** section, click **Manage site features**.

9. The first feature listed is the **Content Organizer**. Click on the **Activate** button to the right of the feature.

10. Click **Site Actions**, then **Site Settings**.

11. Click **Content Organizer Settings** under the **Site Administration** section.

12. In the section labelled **Submission Points**, copy the web service URL shown.

13. Open the **Central Administration** screen and click **General Application Settings**.

14. The first section is **External Service Connections**. Under it, click **Configure send to connections**.

15. In the section labeled Connection Settings, set the following parameters in the display as follows:

   - Copy the URL from step 12 into the **Send to URL** text box.
   - Ensure that the **Allow manual submission...** checkbox is not checked.
   - Enter **Display name** as **Route Documents**.

16. Click **Add Connection**.

17. Navigate back to SharePoint website A.

18. Click **Site Actions**, then **Site Settings**.

19. Click **Content Organizer Rules**.

20. Hover over the item named **CashFlow** and click **Edit Item**.

21. The following screen pops up:

Choose the **Another content organizer in a different site** option and select **Route Documents** from the drop-down.

Click **OK**.

22. Follow steps from 9 to 12 from the first recipe.

23. Navigate to the **Drop Off Library** in SharePoint Site B. The document will be present there.

How it works...

The key to this recipe is that both sites need to have the Content Organizer feature activated; steps 1 to 9 accomplish this.

Included in those steps was designating SharePoint Site A as having the capability to provide documents to another site. We did this in step 4.

The next part of getting routing between sites to work was to configure the connections between the two sites. SharePoint Site A was the provider and SharePoint Site B was the consumer. Central Administration acts as the glue needed to wire up the connection between these two sites.

Steps 10 to 16 accomplished the wiring. Copying the URL from Site A, we created a connection through Central Administration.

Then we edited the Content Organizer rule from the first recipe and changed the location in the drop-down for the destination. The new location (Route Documents) appeared in the drop-down as result of the changes we did in the Central Administration.

As we routed the document, SharePoint provided confirmation, including a link to the new location where the document was routed.

There's more...

When going to Central Administration to modify the Send to Connections option, please be cognizant as to the web application showing. The list is maintained on a web application basis. Documents can be routed to different web applications.

Configuring content deployment

Publishing information is a critical mission in many organizations—large or small. Companies of all sizes can effectively leverage the output of information to communicate a positive message to their investors, customers, vendors, and employees.

This is normally the job of the communications group in an enterprise organization. In smaller companies, this job is typically done by IT, even if the business is creating the content. Reasons for this may be ownership of the web server machine to understanding how to put together an HTML page.

SharePoint 2010 content deployment gets everyone in the organization involved, except for IT (outside of configuration), which is a liberating experience for users. It ensures that IT is no longer a bottleneck.

Content deployment moves data from a source site to a destination site without any interference. It is critical to define and configure where the data goes.

In this recipe, we will configure and set up a content deployment job.

Getting ready

You must have farm-level administrative permissions to the Central Administration site.

Configure two web applications prior to beginning this recipe. They are:

- ▶ WebAppS: This is the source web application
- ▶ WebAppD: This is the destination web application

Create the following Team Site structure:

- ▶ Create a Site collection under WebAppS
- ▶ Create the following team sites under that site collection:
    - ❑ SiteA
    - ❑ Create a subsite called SiteAa
    - ❑ SiteB
    - ❑ SiteC

How to do it...

1. Open the **Central Administration** screen and click **General Application Settings**.
2. Click **Configure Content Deployment**.
3. A new page is displayed with six sections:
   - **Accept Content Deployment Jobs**: choose **Accept incoming...**
   - **Import Server**: Select **Destination Server**.
   - **Export Server**: Select **Source Server**.
   - **Connection Security**: Retain the default encryption.
   - **Temporary Files**: Retain the default setting.
   - **Reporting**: Retain the default setting.

   Click **OK**.
4. Click **Application Management**.
5. Under the second section named **Site Collections**, click **Create site collections**.
6. Click `WebAppD` for **Web Application**.
7. Fill in the other fields appropriately, except **Template Selection**. For this option choose the **Custom** tab and leave < **Select template later...** > as selected.

   Click **OK**.
8. Click **General Application Settings**. Under the **Content Deployment** section, click **Configure content deployment**.
9. Click **New Path**.
10. Fill in the following on the ensuing page:
    - Name of Content Deploy job: CD to Dest.
    - Source web application.
    - Destination Central Administration Server with Port number. You must type this in the format: `http://servername:port#`.
    - Enter in the Authentication Info.

    Click the **Connect** button.
11. After the connection is successful, you can enter the **Destination –WebAppD** and / as the **Destination site collection**. Leave the other options as default.

    Click **OK**.

12. Create the job by clicking **Create Job** in the drop-down list as show in the following screenshot:

13. On the ensuing page, modify the following:

  ❑ **Name**: Enter a name for the job

  ❑ **Scope**: To select scope:

    ▸ Choose **Specific....**

    ▸ Click on the **Select Sites** button.

    ▸ The following screenshot appears:

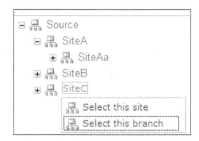

    ▸ For **SiteA**, choose **Select this branch**.

    ▸ For **SiteC**, choose **Select this site**.

Click **OK**.

  ❑ **Frequency**: Check the box for the **Run this job...**option.

  ❑ **Notification**: Check both boxes and enter an e-mail address.

Click **OK**.

14. Hover over the newly created job **CD to Dest** and choose **Run Now** from the drop-down list.

How it works...

The first thing to understand about content deployment is that the source and destination cannot be in the same database. The simplest way around this is to create two web applications, as was done as per the requirements of this recipe.

Content deployment extracts the data from the source content database as an XML file. Another process imports the XML file and extracts it onto the destination content database.

The reason behind choosing the **<Select template later...>** option when setting up a destination site collection is that the first time content deploy is run, all assets are transported to the destination site. This includes even the site template. Of course that template must be available in the destination site or the job will fail.

Ensuing jobs only deploy changes since the last successful run. Next a path is set up, which is simply a mapping between the source and the destination site collections. Once the mapping (path) is in place, a job can be set up. This was done in steps 12 and 13.

Finally a job was manually run in step 14. The outcome of this job should be a new Team Site collection with only SiteA and SiteC available.

There's more...

When assigning the path, you may get the following error:

Type the URL of the destination Central Administration Server:

Either the URL for the destination Web application is not valid, or you do not have permissions to the Central Administration site on the destination server farm.

Error details: The remote Web service request failed with this message : 'Client found response content type of 'text/html; charset=utf-8', but expected 'text/xml'. '.

A possible reason for this error is that both the source and destination site collections reside in the same content database under the same web application. The content deployment process cannot create a new item in the destination using the same GUIDs as the source.

The solution is to deploy to another web application.

Adding a Content Type hub

A Content Type hub is a feature that publishes content types to other site collections. In SharePoint 2010, the content type can be defined once and managed from a central location. No longer is the content type creation in a site collection a silo of work that must be repeated in all the other site collections (and web applications) where it must be available.

Content types can now be shared across an organization.

The business rationale for this feature is the ability for an organization to create a central repository of content type assets. Then, as other site collections need to leverage these content types, they are available.

A popular feature is the publishing website. It is not uncommon to create different article content types that contain site columns. Enterprise organizations would leverage the article content types across site collections so that they are consuming the same metadata. The effect of this is a highly efficient organization through the reuse of content structures. Everyone is speaking the same language, even if there are nuances to the organization's vernacular.

This recipe shows how to set up a Content Type hub.

Getting ready

You must have farm-level administrative permissions to the Central Administration site.

Create a site collection called `sites\ContentTypeHub`, based on the Publishing Site Template, and make yourself the owner.

The Document ID service must be activated on the site collection that is the Content Type hub in order for the publishing to work.

How to do it...

1. Open the **Central Administration** screen and click **Application Management**.
2. The third section is **Service Applications**. Under this section, click **Manage service applications**.
3. Find the **Managed Metadata Service** application and left-click to the right of the name, the line will be highlighted.
4. Click the **Properties** option on the ribbon.
5. The **Create New Managed Metadata Service** pop-up screen will appear. At the bottom of the pop-up screen, you can see a box to enter the URL of the Content Type hub.

Enter the URL of the site collection (Content Type hub) from which this service application will consume content types.

Content Type hub

☐ Report syndication import errors from Site Collections using this service application.

6. Enter the URL of the site collection that was created prior to the beginning of this recipe. It should be of the form `http://servername/sites/ContentTypeHub`.

7. Check the **Report syndication...** option and click **OK**.

8. Click to the right of **Managed Metadata Service connection**, highlighting the line. Click the **Properties** option on the ribbon.

9. The **Edit Managed Metadata Service Connection** pop-up appears. Check the **Consumes content types from the Content Type...** option; the other three options are checked by default.

Select the settings for this Managed Metadata Service Connection.

☑ This service application is the default storage location for Keywords.

☑ This service application is the default storage location for column specific term sets.

☑ Consumes content types from the Content Type Gallery at http://2008server/sites/ContentTypeHub.

☑ Push-down Content Type Publishing updates from the Content Type Gallery to sub-sites and lists using the content type.

Click **OK**.

10. Open the `sites/ContentTypeHub` site collection. Click **Site Actions** and then **Site Settings**.

11. Under the **Galleries** section click **Site columns**.

12. Click **Create**. In the **Name** column, call it ArticleHeadline. Keep it as a single line of text and keep the rest of the defaults. Press **OK**.

13. Navigate back to **Site Settings**. Under the **Galleries** section, click **Site content types**.

14. Click **Create**. In the **Name** column, enter **Article**.

15. Click on the drop-down for **Parent Content Type** and choose **Publishing Content Types** from the **Select parent content type from:** drop-down. Click **OK**.

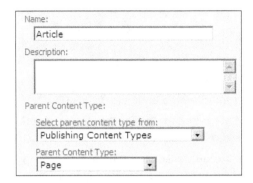

16. A page called Site Content Type Information is presented. Click **Add from existing site columns**.

17. Add article headline and click **OK**.

18. Click **Manage publishing for this content type**.

19. By default **Publish** is chosen. Click **OK**.

20. Create a new Site Collection called `sites/ContentTypeHubConsume`, through Central Administration. Base it on the Publishing Portal Template.

21. Now, when the timer job runs, the new article content type that we just created (`ContentTypeHubConsume`) will automatically be published to the new site collection.

How it works...

The first ten steps in the recipe identify and configure the Content Hub Type site collection in the Managed Metadata Service. All of the content types are published from this hub.

In our example, both site collections were created under one web application. The web application is associated with the Managed Metadata Service that was modified in step 3.

The rest of the recipe was spent creating a content type called Article. Clicking on the content type in the **Site Content Types Gallery** shows a new menu item called **Manage publishing for this content type** under **Settings**.

Settings

- Name, description, and group
- Advanced settings
- Workflow settings
- Delete this site content type
- Manage publishing for this content type

This option contains a section called **Publishing History** that shows when the content type was last published. It contains three radio options: **Publishing**, **Unpublish**, and **Republish**.

It is important that steps 18 and 19 be run as the content type will not be published until these steps are completed.

When publishing a content type, it is not immediately available in the other site collections. This is because there are two jobs that must be run. The first is called **Content Type Hub** and it publishes the content types that need to be pushed. The second job is called **Content Type Subscriber** and it puts the available content types in the site collections.

There's more...

In the site collection, which is the **Content Type Hub** under **Site Settings**, there are two menu items under Site Collection Administration. These are:

- ▸ **Content type publishing**: This setting allows the administrator to refresh all of the published content types. It contains a link to the error log and shows the hubs for all existing Managed Metadata Service applications.

- ▸ **Content type service application type error log**: In step 7 of the recipe, we enabled the **Report syndication...** checkbox, in order for us to be able to receive reports on import errors. These errors are found in this log.

Site collections that are not Content Type Hubs, have only the first menu item—**Content type publishing**.

Managing External Content Types

An External Content Type is SharePoint's way to access the back end data in another data source. This could be the ERP, CRM, or custom manufacturing system. The data is defined in a database and now the organization wants to consume that data through SharePoint.

In order to consume the data, we need to define the properties of that data to SharePoint. This is done by creating an **External Content Type** (**ECT**). This is an XML file that defines and identifies the object.

Typically, an administrator does not create the External Content Types. Creation is done by power users or developers through SharePoint Designer and Business Connectivity Services. However, it is important to be able to manage these entities as an administrator.

This recipe will show how to identify the External Content Types on the farm and how to set permissions.

Getting ready

You must have farm-level administrative permissions to the Central Administration site. You should also have an external content type already implemented.

How to do it...

1. Open the **Central Administration** screen and click **Application Management**.

2. The third section is **Service Applications**. Under this section, click **Manage service applications**.

3. Find the **Business Data Connectivity Service** application proxy and click on it.

4. The page lists all of the External Content Types. The ribbon shows the following:

5. Click the box to the right of the listed External Content Types you wish to modify.

6. Click the **Set Object Permissions** option on the ribbon.

7. Add a user to the following pop-up dialog:

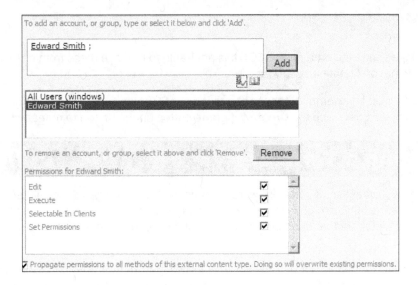

To add an account, or group, type or select it below and click 'Add'.

Edward Smith ;

Add

All Users (windows)
Edward Smith

To remove an account, or group, select it above and click 'Remove'. | Remove

Permissions for Edward Smith:

☑ Edit
☑ Execute
☑ Selectable In Clients
☑ Set Permissions

☑ Propagate permissions to all methods of this external content type. Doing so will overwrite existing permissions.

8. Click **OK**.

How it works...

External Content Types are created with SharePoint Designer 2010. After it is created there is the management of this entity. This is done through Central Administration by the administrator of the service application or Farm Administrator.

The following can be done:

▶ **Obtaining a listing of all of the External Content Types for a BDC service application instance**: This was performed in step 4.

▶ **Setting permission for an External Content Type**: Covered in step 7.

▶ **Deleting an External Content Type**: Achieved using the **Delete** button on the ribbon.

▶ **Viewing details of an External Content Type**: Click on the External Content Type directly. A list of the fields will appear along with any associations, actions, or filters.

▶ **Add an action to an external content type**: This is done by hovering over the ECT and choosing the appropriate action from the drop-down list.

▶ **Define a profile page**: This is achieved with the help of the **Configure** button on the ribbon.

▶ **Creating or updating a profile page for an External Content Type**: This is done with the help of the **Create/Upgrade** button on the ribbon.

A profile page shows the data for the ECT. It is advisable to manage these from one site so that they do not proliferate across your farm.

As the schema on an external database changes, your ECT must reflect these changes. This is not done dynamically. Use the **Create/Upgrade** button on the ribbon to manage this.

Creating a Term Set

A **Term Set** is a collection of pertinent words that define the language your business uses. Term Sets are the language of your business. Every business has its own terminology and this becomes the metadata that enables communication between information workers in the company.

Take the example of a doctor's visit. Typically, there are hundreds of physical folders that contain patient name and history. Forms containing every type of malady, approval, and diagnosis make up these folders. The folders are categorized by name and a specific assigned ID. Doctors give orders to nurses in a language we do not understand (neither can we pronounce). All of this information makes up the health care metadata.

This metadata can come from many places such as defined terminology, folder structures, and forms. The way to structure this for it to be available to a SharePoint system is through the use of Term Sets.

In this recipe, we will show how to utilize the Term Store Management tool to create a term set.

Getting ready

You must have administrative permissions to the Central Administration site and must have the Managed Metadata Finance Service running (it was created in *Chapter 2, Service Applications*).

How to do it...

1. Open the SharePoint 2010 **Central Administration** website.
2. Click **Application Management**.
3. Under the **Service Applications** section, click **Manage service applications**.
4. Click on the **Managed Metadata Finance** service application.
5. Under the Taxonomy Term Store, click the drop-down list next to **Managed Metadata Finance**.

6. Select the **New Group** option from the drop-down list, as shown in the following screenshot:

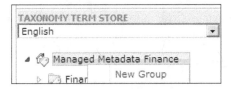

7. Name the group as **Financial Aid**. Leave the other fields blank (**Description**, **Group Managers**, and **Contributors**).
8. Hover over **Financial Aid** and click the drop-down list named **New Term Set**.
9. Name the new Term Set as **Public**. Leave the other fields at their default values.
10. Hover over **Public** and click the drop-down named **Create Term**.
11. Select the **FAFSA** option from the **Create Term** drop-down to get the screen shown here:

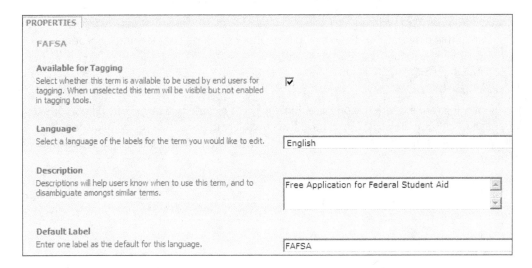

12. Click **Save**.

How it works...

Prior to creating a Term Set, a Term Set Group must be created. The group is necessary to organize and secure a collection of Term Sets. In step 7 of the recipe, we could have assigned Group Managers, or Managers and Contributors, who would be responsible for the group Financial Aid.

When creating a Term Set we create one called Public. In our example of Financial Aid, we are breaking down Financial Aid into Public versus Private. Under Public, we can create a multitude of terms; however, in our example we have created only FAFSA.

This term is available for tagging, which means that end users will see it when classifying metadata. Terms can be nested up to seven times.

An example of this could be as follows:

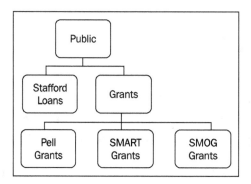

As shown in this diagram, Pell Grants is a term under the term Grants—one level deep.

There's more...

When creating terms, there are often multiple ways to reference a term. This can be due to language or cultural dialects. Terms have the capability to enter synonyms for a term. The following is a screenshot that shows what the field looks like and is part of the properties of the term.

More info

You can add up to 30,000 items in one term set. Each term store allows up to 1,000 term sets.

See also

> ▸ *The Setting up a Managed Metadata Service recipe* from *Chapter 2, Service Applications*

Importing a Term Set

Term Sets can not only be created but can also be imported. As we have discussed, Term Sets define the language of your business. Enterprise organizations typically have so much information (defined metadata) that creating a Term Set manually is not a preferable option.

Using a comma-separated values (CSV) file, this metadata can be imported to the system up to seven levels deep.

Using the provided `FinancialAidTermSet.csv` file, this recipe will show you how to create a Term Set outside of the Term Set Management Tool and import it.

Getting ready

You must have administrative permissions to the Central Administration site and have the Managed Metadata Finance Service created in Chapter 2. You also need to have the `FinancialAidTermSet.csv` file loaded in your directory.

How to do it...

1. Open the SharePoint 2010 **Central Administration** website.
2. Click **Application Management**.
3. Under the **Service Applications** section, click **Manage service applications**.
4. Click on the **Managed Metadata Finance** service application.
5. Under the Taxonomy Term Store, hover over the group titled **Financial Aid**. Click the drop-down list by the name **Import Term Set**.
6. Choose the file on the ensuing pop-up window and click **OK**.

7. A confirmation will be shown, informing us that the Term Set has been imported. A successful import looks like the following screenshot:

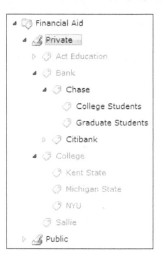

How it works...

The Term Set CSV file is broken down as follows (by position):

- Term Set Name
- Description of Term Set
- Locale Identifier (LCID)
- Available for tagging (TRUE or FALSE)
- Term Description
- Level N Term (Levels 1 through 7)

The Term Set must have as its first line:

```
Term Set Name,Term Set Description,LCID,Available for Tagging,Term
Description,Level 1 Term,Level 2 Term,Level 3 Term,Level 4 Term,Level
5 Term,Level 6 Term,Level 7 Term
Company Enterprise Taxonomy,Enterprise taxonomy for Corp
Inc.,,TRUE,,,,,,,,
```

There's more...

Term Sets cannot be exported via the interface or object model.

See also

▸   *Creating a Term Set*

In place Records Management

Records Management no longer exists only in the Records Center in SharePoint 2010; it is present throughout SharePoint libraries and lists. A document can be declared a record no matter which library it is found in.

Once a document is declared as a record, organizational policies can applied. Due to the oversight of entities such as Sarbanes-Oxley, DOD certification, ISO certification, among others, it is imperative that organizations manage a document from cradle to grave. The administrator should be aware that this depends on the requirements of the governing body. It is not realistic to believe that SharePoint 2010 meets every certification need out of the box.

We also live in a society of litigation, which means every piece of information in an organization is subject to scrutiny. Records Management helps the administrator to be proactive to these type of initiatives when they happen. Records Management is how we manage what happens to a document. This recipe will go through how to enable and declare a record.

Getting ready

Set up a team site prior to performing this recipe. You must be a site collection owner of the team site where records will be declared.

How to do it...

1. Navigate to the team site. Click **Site Actions** and then **Site Settings**.

2. Under the **Site Collection Administration** section, click **Site collection features**.

3. Locate the **In Place Records Management** feature and click on the **Activate** button.

4. Navigate back to **Site Settings**.

5. Click the new menu item named **Record declaration settings** under **Site Collection Administration**.

6. Fill in the required details on the ensuing page.

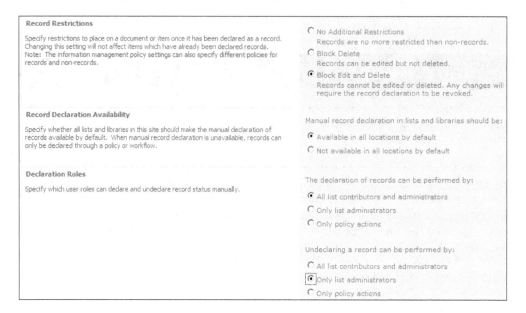

Click **OK**.

7. Click **Shared Documents** and upload a document to the library if one does not exist.

8. Hover over the document and click on the drop-down item **Compliance Details**.

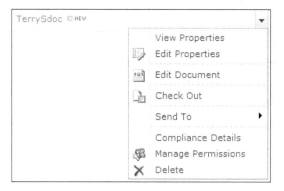

9. The following pop-up screen appears:

Event	Action	Recurrence	Scheduled occurence date
This item is not subject to a retention policy			
Name	Auditing_settings_2010-07-18T230744.xlsx		
Content Type	Document		
Folder Path	Shared Documents		
Exemption Status	Not Exempt You cannot exempt/unexempt item from policy.		
Hold Status	Not on hold You cannot add/remove item from hold.		
Record Status	Not a record Declare as a record		
Audit Log	Generate audit log report		

Click on the **Declare as a record** link.

10. You will get a pop-up window asking your permission to lock down an item for editing. Click **OK**.

11. The record is processed and is now shown with a lock on the file icon, as seen in the following screenshot:

How it works...

As shown in the recipe, documents stay in their original location when declared as a record. They do not need to be routed to a central location such as Records Center. In the prior recipe, we saw how routing works.

In place Records Management is enabled at the site collection level, as shown in step 3. This brought us a new menu item pick that was configured in step 6. There were three sections that allow the configuration of managing records.

The first section, **Record Restrictions**, pertains to the editing and deletion of records. The second section is for the manual declaration of records. If this is marked as **Not Available...**, then a workflow or policy must be configured to declare a record. This would be done through the use of managed metadata.

The last section pertains to the permissions of who can do what. In the recipe shown, all could declare a record but only list administrators could undeclare a record.

There's more...

While the configuration for declaring records was shown at the site collection level, it can be overridden at the document library level.

Do this by navigating to the document library and clicking on the document library settings on the ribbon. There is a **Record declaration settings** menu item under **Permissions and Management**.

Clicking on this brings up the following page:

Manual Record Declaration Availability	
Specify whether this list should allow the manual declaration of records. When manual record declaration is unavailable, records can only be declared through a policy or workflow.	⦿ Use the site collection default setting: Allow the manual declaration of records ○ Always allow the manual declaration of records ○ Never allow the manual declaration of records
Automatic Declaration	
Specify whether all items should become records when added to this list.	☐ Automatically declare items as records when they are added to this list.

Clicking **OK** overrides the site collection settings.

More info

In step 9, we used the Compliance menu item in the document drop-down list to declare the document as a record.

Another way to accomplish this would be to check the box next to the document, click **Documents** under **Library Tools** on the ribbon. There is a button (which has a drop-down list associated) called **Declare Record**.

It is more efficient to use this when there is a need to declare more than one document as a record.

9
Social Architecture

In this chapter, we will cover:

- ▸ Setting up a tag cloud and navigating to the Term Store
- ▸ Disabling social features for a user
- ▸ Deleting a note associated with a page
- ▸ Viewing an Activity feed
- ▸ Setting up and compiling an audience
- ▸ Creating a synchronization connection
- ▸ Changing import/export for user profiles
- ▸ Adding a user subtype for user profile
- ▸ Creating a new user profile property

Introduction

SharePoint 2010 has been architected to be socially functional, which allows people to collaborate and utilize socialization components similar to Facebook, Twitter, and other social sites.

The business proposition of this functionality being that the information in the organization is uncovered faster and shared quickly. Components, such as rating an item, are automatically shared by users, and the value of that item is decided by the user base.

The value is determined by increased participation in deciding which information in the SharePoint system is relevant. Better information results in better decision making, which has a positive effect on the return on investment. Elements of the SharePoint social experience can be categorized as:

▶ **Profile and context**: The **profile** part defines the elements that make up a user. Simple things such as birthday, work anniversary day, interests, skills, and phone number.

The second part, the **context** part, defines the location of the user and time of activities in which they are participating. Together, this provides a 360-degree view of a user.

Consider the following example to realize the power of this information. A manager can now be notified in their newsfeed when an event is about to occur for any of their employees. The manager can then act on that information in a proactive fashion, making the employee feel valued, which in turn will result in an improved performance from the employee.

▶ **Content**: This includes documents, links, and other assets. It includes what the user keeps personal versus what the user shares with the organization.

▶ **User's relationships**: This involves answering the following questions:

   ❑ Who does the person work for?

   ❑ Who reports to him/her?

It includes quickly assessing where that individual fits into the structure of the organization.

▶ **Activities**: We try and answer the following questions here:

   ❑ What does this person like?

   ❑ What information are they tagging?

   ❑ What type of tags do they use?

   ❑ What type of comments are they making about the information?

All of these elements are found in SharePoint, in the My Sites, tagging, ratings, targeted content, profile information, and Activity feeds. This chapter will explore some basic recipes that can be expanded as the organization becomes comfortable with SharePoint.

Setting up a tag cloud and navigating to the Term Store

Social tagging is a feature of SharePoint 2010 that brings immediate business value. As your users traverse sites, they have the ability to tag pages with the help of the **I Like It** button, found in the upper right corner of a page. At the same time, other users of the same sites can tag pages.

SharePoint uses tags as a way to help users describe content. As users of a site tag information, these tags accrue as metadata. A database of this metadata is kept within SharePoint. With the new managed metadata service, a user can begin typing in a new tag and a list of suggestions will appear. Users can then either use a suggested tag or create one of their own.

Using a tag cloud, the web part allows the user to see all their tags, and each tag is presented as a link to the associated content. This becomes a navigational component.

In this recipe, we will see how to set up a tag cloud and the associated Term Store it consumes. This will give you, as an administrator, knowledge about how managed metadata interfaces with the tag cloud.

Getting ready

You must have a team site set up and should be the owner. The managed metadata service should be set up and functional. You must have farm-level administrative permissions to the Central Administration site.

How to do it...

1. Navigate to your team site homepage.
2. Click the **Page** option above the ribbon (to the right of the **Browse** button).
3. Position the cursor on the page where the tag cloud will be placed. Click **Edit** on the ribbon.
4. Click **Insert**. Then click **Web Part** on the ribbon.
5. Select **Social Collaboration** under **Categories** and select **Tag Cloud** under **Web Parts**, as shown in the following screenshot:

6. Click **Add**.

7. Click **Page** and then click **Save** on the ribbon.

8. The tag cloud appears on the page and should look similar to the following screenshot:

9. Open the **Central Administration** screen and click **Application Management**.

10. The third section is **Service Applications**. Under this section, click **Manage service applications**.

11. Find the **Managed Metadata Service** application and left-click to the right of the name—the line will be highlighted.

12. Click **Manage** on the ribbon. The Taxonomy Term Store is presented.

13. Add a user under the Term Store Administrators. Do this by typing in the domain/username and clicking the **Check User** control. You can also use the **Address Book Search** control to the right of the **Check User** control.

14. Click **Save**.

15. Click the drop-down list to the left of **System** and then to the left of **Keywords**. There should be a screen similar to the following screenshot:

How it works...

The tag cloud social feature relies upon two architectural components being set up within SharePoint—the user profile service and the managed metadata service. *Chapter 2, Service Applications*, showed how to set up the managed metadata service.

The first part of the recipe (steps 1–8) adds the tag cloud to a page. As we can see in the screenshot of step 8, several terms immediately show up. One of these terms, EBITDA, relates to *Chapter 4, Site Administration*.

Steps 9–15 show us how to navigate back to the Term Store to see from where they originate. In particular, the **sample** term is shown in the managed metadata taxonomy. This is the term that is surfaced in the tag cloud.

In the *Term Store management recipe* from Chapter 4, we saw how to manage a Term Store, which included how to create terms.

The result of these two halves builds a complete picture, showing the full life-cycle of a term, from the store to the tag cloud.

There's more...

The **I Like It** button at the top of the page allows a user to automatically tag a page. When this is done, **I Like It** is added to the System Term Store as part of the folksonomy.

The button to the right, **Tags & Notes**, allows a user to tag a page with their own tag and create a public note. This is shown in the following screenshot:

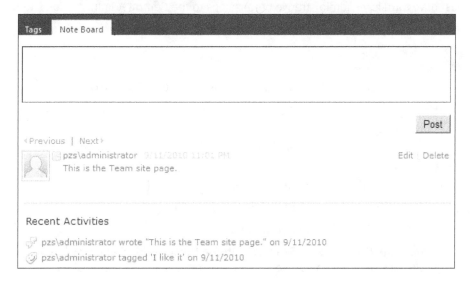

▶ The *Setting up Managed Metadata Service* recipe from *Chapter 2, Service Applications*

▶ The *Term Store management* recipe from *Chapter 4, Site Administration*

Disabling social features for a user

One of the key features of SharePoint 2010 is social components. These components are enabled by default. However, we do not always want users adding tags, using the Note Board and other social features. Organizations might need to turn them off for a particular user or even a group.

Take the case where an organization has a site set up for their vendors to use and exchange information. It may not make sense, from a business perspective, for the users of this site to be tagging items and using the **I Like It** feature. They are providing information to an organization through the extranet site. They are not looking to do things like rate the information on the site.

In a case like this, the social features can be disabled for that group. In this recipe, we will see how to accomplish this.

Getting ready

You must have farm-level administrative permissions to the Central Administration site.

How to do it...

1. Open the **Central Administration** screen and click **Application Management**.
2. The third section is **Service Applications**. Under this section, click **Manage service applications**.
3. Find **User Profile Service Application** and left-click to the right of the name— the line will be highlighted.
4. Click the **Manage** option on the ribbon.
5. In the **People** section, click **Manage User Permissions**.
6. Click on the line that says **All Authenticated Users**.
7. Uncheck the **Use Personal Features**, **Create Personal Site**, and **Use Social Features** checkboxes. The screen should look similar to the following screenshot:

8. Click **OK**.

How it works...

Using Central Administration, the recipe shows how to navigate to the User Profile Service management page. There is no direct way to get to the page; it must be done with the help of the service application as shown in steps 1 to 4.

Once there, the section **People** contains the link to permissions, where the social features can be disabled.

Step 7 shows the screen that contains three items per user/group:

▶ **Use Personal Features**: These are items such as **My Profile**.

▶ **Create Personal Site**: When unchecked, the user will also not be able to provision a personal site—commonly known as My Site.

▶ **Use Social Features**: The user cannot use the social features that are part of the SharePoint 2010 project. Items such as the **I Like It** and **Notes** button are removed.

Now groups can be created that do not need to have these types of services, for instance, auditors that need access to the system but are not part of the ecosystem of a company. These types of resources are typically only onsite for a short duration with a focus on controls.

An administrator must be careful and cognizant to understand that a user may belong to several groups. Therefore, if the permission is deleted from one group, users may still have access via another group.

In this recipe, all of the features were removed; you could pick and choose specific features for the groups that exist.

There's more...

There is a way to disable the I Like It and Notes at the farm level. This is done through a feature called `SocialRibbonControl`. Be aware that doing this will also disable other social features such as ratings. While this can be done through the UI, the simplest way to disable these social features is through PowerShell. This can be achieved using the following command:

```
Disable-SPFeature -Identity <SocialRibbonControl>
```

Deleting a note associated with a page

Notes associated with tags are powerful as they expose comments of other users to the user community of that portal. The implication of this capability is that users can give information about a page or object and have others view it.

A possible shortcoming of this capability is that company information can possibly be exposed to the people who are not supposed to access it.

Consider the example of product pages. Product pages can be viewed by the whole company and may be rated as new products are developed. This is a powerful feature of SharePoint's new social features.

However, in rating the product, a person may mistakenly put financial information on the Note Board that is exposed publicly within the company. In an enterprise with hundreds or even thousands of products, this information could possibly be exposed for a while.

SharePoint 2010 has a feature where the Farm Administrator can search all the Note Boards for particular information. This recipe shows how that is achieved.

Getting ready

You must have a team site set up and should be the owner. The managed metadata service should be set up and functional. You must have farm-level administrative permissions to the Central Administration site.

How to do it...

1. Navigate to your team site homepage.
2. Click **Tags & Notes** in the upper right-hand corner of the site.
3. In the dialog that appears, click the **Note Board** tab.
4. Enter the following into the text box: **Project Meteor, which we all know is the new product, Starlight, looks great.**
5. Click **Post**. The screen should look like the following screenshot:

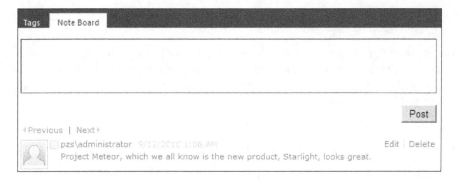

Close the dialog box.

6. Open the Central Administration screen and click **Application Management**.

7. The third section is **Service Applications**. Under this section, click **Manages service applications**.

8. Find **User Profile Service Application** and left-click to the right of the name— the line will be highlighted.

9. Under the **My Site Settings** section, click **Manage Social Tags and Notes**.

10. Fill in the form as shown:

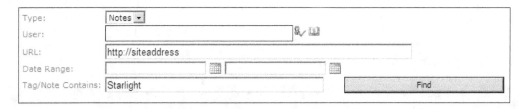

- In the **Type** drop-down list, change the value from **Tags** to **Notes**.
- Enter **Starlight** in the **Tag/Note Contains** text box.

11. Click **Find**.

12. A listing of any note containing the word **Starlight** appears. Click the checkbox to the left of the note.

13. Click **Delete**. A confirmation pop-up window appears. Click **Yes**.

How it works...

In the recipe, **Starlight** is the name of the new product not yet released, but it was viewable on the company intranet. Someone put the name of the new product on the Note Board. There are a number of reasons, from a business point of view, why a company would not want this information to be released before a company announcement.

In the recipe, tracking the product name down by URL, we were able to locate every instance of this name and quickly delete the note references.

Notes are public by default. This should be noted in the governance policy of the organization.

There's more...

Tags can also be found and deleted if they are not acceptable. Unlike notes, tags can be made private to a user. After creating the tag, check the box marked **Private**.

Now the tag will only be visible to the user.

Viewing an Activity feed

In SharePoint 2010, Activity feeds give SharePoint users the ability to know what their colleagues are doing. A user will track only those colleagues that they are interested in following, which reduces the organization noise.

You can also receive updates in the Newsfeed of your My Site when your colleagues add tags to documents and pages. Also, if you are following a keyword as an interest, you can receive an update when anyone applies that tag to content that you have permission to view.

Every update that occurs is configurable by the user. In this way, users see only those things that they are interested in. In this recipe, we will see where to make these updates.

Getting ready

You must have a My Site set up.

How to do it...

1. Open a team site.

2. Navigate to the upper right-hand corner and click the drop-down list to the right of your name. In the following screenshot, the name is **System Account**:

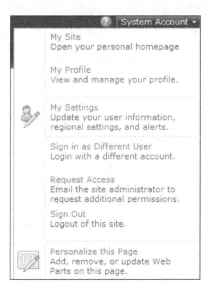

3. Click the **My Site** link.

4. There will be three navigational links under the **What's New** section. Click **Newsfeed Settings**.

5. There are three sections under **Newsfeed Settings**:

   □ **Interests**: This is a text box in which you can type in activities outside of work. If someone else has the same interest, there is type-ahead capability.

   □ **Email Notifications**: You will be notified via e-mails, at regular intervals, about the list of activities that are followed by you.

   □ **Activities I am following**: This list contains all the activities in which you wish to be notified.

6. Click **Save and Close**.

How it works...

Activity feeds are part of the SharePoint 2010 My Sites. A My Site consists of three components as seen in the following screenshot:

- ▶ **My Newsfeed**: This is the Activity feed.
- ▶ **My Content**: This is where information such as documents, pictures, and pages is stored.
- ▶ **My Profile:** This contains the information about items you have tagged, where you fit in the organization, peers, and other sites where you have membership.

There are two types of Activity feeds:

- ▶ **Consolidated**: This is what the user tracks and is shown on their My Newsfeed page.
- ▶ **Published**: These are the user's activities. This is on the My Profile page.

In step 5, it was requested that the user put in any activities that they want their colleagues to know about. The reason behind the type-ahead feature working so efficiently is that the information is saved in the managed metadata service system's Term Store.

This is referred to as the folksonomy. This assists in keeping a common terminology in the organization.

There's more...

Newsfeeds can be consumed by other readers. For example, Outlook 2010 can consume RSS feeds. The following are examples of the links to use (your links will probably be different):

- ▶ **Consolidated**: `http://mysite/_layouts/activityfeed.aspx?consolidated=true`
- ▶ **Published**: `http://mysite/_layouts/activityfeed.aspx?publisher=<accountname>`

More info

As an administrator, it is important to understand that there are three service applications functionally integrated with Activity feeds:

- ▶ Search
- ▶ User profile
- ▶ Managed Metadata Service

Setting up and compiling an audience

Audiences are a brilliant way to target content to specific users. Typically, users are in Organizational Units (OU) in Active Directory (AD). This is a way for enterprises to classify the role of an individual in the organization.

A role can be classified by where a person is located—for example, North America, Asia, Europe, and so on. Or the person can be classified by type of employment such as hourly or salary.

Once classified at the AD level, audiences can be applied to a SharePoint audience. Once an audience is created and compiled, it can be applied as a parameter in web parts functionally targeting that content.

This recipe reviews how to create an audience.

Getting ready

You must have farm-level administrative permissions to the Central Administration site. Set up an OU group named na_hourly in AD (user profile sync must be run for this to be available).

How to do it...

1. Open the **Central Administration** screen and click **Application Management**.
2. The third section is **Service Applications**. Under this section, click **Manage service applications**.
3. Find **User Profile Service Application**. Left-click to the right of the name—the line will be highlighted. This will open the user profile management section
4. Under the section named **People**, click **Manage Audiences**.
5. Click **New Audience**.
6. The following page is displayed. Fill in the fields as shown:

Use this page to create an audience. Then add rules to identify matching users.

* Indicates a required field

Properties

Type a unique and identifiable name and description for this audience.

Specify whether you want users to be included in the audience that satisfy all the rules of this audience or any of the rules of this audience.

Name: *
NAHourly
Example: Sales Managers
Description:
North American Hourly Workers

Owner:
PZS\administrator ;

Include users who:
* Satisfy all of the rules
* Satisfy any of the rules

Click **OK**.

7. The page to add a rule is now displayed. Fill it the details as shown:

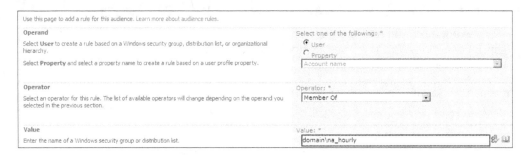

- ❏ **Operand**: Select User
- ❏ **Operator**: Select Member Of
- ❏ **Value**: Type the name of the Active Directory group that you created—domain/na_hourly

Click OK.

8. The **Audience Properties** page is displayed. Click **Compile audience** under that section.

How it works...

Audiences have a dependency on the user profile service application being configured and operational.

As seen in step 7, a rule can be set up for either a User or Property parameter. The recipe discussed here uses the User parameter. The operator is dependent on the aforementioned parameter. As User has been chosen here as the parameter, there are two possibilities:

- ▶ **Reports Under**: This is a UserID—typically a manager of some type. Using this is an indication that AD and the properties are configured.
- ▶ **Member Of**: Allows the use of a windows security group or distribution list.

Choosing Property as operand changes the value of Operator as well as of the Value setting. The first decision to be made should be which user property to choose. The operator consists of the values shown in the following screenshot:

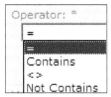

Finally, a value is chosen that is part of the domain.

This illuminates the two types of audiences in SharePoint 2010:

- **Global audiences:** Property under the Operand setting. This is creating a rule based on the properties in the user profile. Elements are set, but as will be shown in another recipe, the administrator can create an element based on need.

- **Windows Security Groups and distribution lists:** User parameter under the Operand setting. This is creating a rule based on security groups and distribution lists. The creation of these items is not typically done by a SharePoint Administrator.

It has been stated many times, but still is crucial enough to be repeated again: the use of audiences does not secure data. With a link, users can navigate to content that is not meant to be seen by them.

There's more...

Using the user profile navigation that was shown in this recipe, audiences can be managed. The following screenshot shows the audience that was created and information about it such as **Last Compiled** and **Description**.

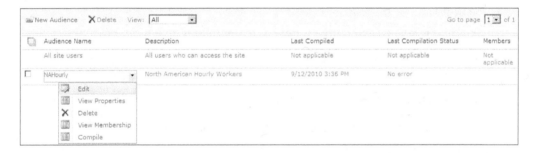

Furthermore, by hovering over the audience, there is a drop-down that helps with the following operations:

- **Edit**: Name, description, and owner of the audience can be changed, except the rule. After clicking OK, the screen with the operand is shown under the section audience rules. Clicking on operand here will allow you to modify the rule.

- **View Properties**: This navigates to the properties of the audience. Here, the administrator can get particular information about the audience such as Create Time. Also, all of the options in the drop-down list are available here.

- **Delete**: Administrator can delete the audience.

- **View Membership**: This is a screen of the members of this audience.

- **Compile**: Allows the administrator to compile the audience.

More info

Under the People section in the user profile service application, there is a link called Schedule Audience compilation. Here a schedule can be set up to compile audiences. In this way, the newest changes are kept up to date.

This is especially important when using security groups and distribution lists. A SharePoint Administrator is not privy to changes in the AD (typically). However, by running the compilation on a schedule, the audiences will be kept current.

Creating a synchronization connection

User Profile Synchronization synchronizes directory or business system information with the SharePoint store. This is a two-way sync. However, you must decide whether a specific user profile property will be exported or imported. By default, user profile properties are configured to be imported.

Once this information is imported, it can be utilized in audiences and the social experience, for example, the Silverlight Organization browser found under My Profile.

SharePoint can sync with the following:

- ▶ Active Directory Domain Services
- ▶ Novell eDirectory version 8.7.3 (LDAP)
- ▶ SunOne version 5.2
- ▶ IBM Tivoli 5.2
- ▶ Business Data Connectivity Service (BCS)

In this recipe, we will set up a connection and start synchronization.

Getting ready

You must have farm-level administrative permissions to the Central Administration site. The User Profile Synchronization service should be started.

How to do it...

1. Open the **Central Administration** screen and click **Application Management**.
2. The third section is **Service Applications**. Under this section, click **Manage service applications**.
3. Find **User Profile Service Application** and click on the name of the service. This will open the **User Profile Management** section.
4. Under the **Synchronization** section, click **Configure Synchronization Connections**.
5. Click **Create New Connection**.

6. The following page is displayed:

Connection Name	
Type	Active Directory

Connection Settings
For the Active Directory directory service server, type in **Forest name** and **Domain controller name**.
 	
For Active Directory connections to work, this account must have directory sync rights.
	Forest name:
	
	○ Auto discover domain controller
	○ Specify a domain controller:
	   Domain controller name:
	
	Authentication Provider Type:
	Windows Authentication
	Authentication Provider Instance:
	
	Account name: *
	
	  Example: DOMAIN\user_name
	Password: *
	
	Confirm password: *
	
	Port:
	389
	☐ Use SSL-secured connection:

Containers Choose which containers you want to be synchronized.	Populate Containers

Fill in the required information.

- ❑ **Connection Name: ADUsers**.

- ❑ **Type: Active Directory**.

- ❑ **Forest name**: Enter the name of your forest (that is, domain.com).

- ❑ **Authentication Provider Type: Windows Authentication** (by default).

- ❑ **Account name**: This should be in the form of domain/administrator.

- ❑ **Password**: Type in the password required to access the account.

- ❑ **Confirm password**: Confirm the password you have typed in the **Password** field.

7. Click **Populate Containers**.

8. Click the OU container that contains the account you want to import. Do no click **Select All**.

9. Click **OK**.

10. Navigate back to User Profile Administration.

11. Under the **Synchronization** section, click **Start Profile Synchronization**.

12. If this is not the first time synchronization is being run, ensure that the **Start Incremental Synchronization** radio button is chosen on the synchronization page. Click **OK**.

How it works...

Synchronization is the process of updating profile information in SharePoint from a directory or business application. SharePoint 2010 has a functional process that accomplishes this task.

Synchronization functionality relies on timer jobs. The User Profile Service must be started in order for the jobs to run properly.

The timer jobs let the User Profile Service interface with three databases:

- ▸ Social DB
- ▸ Profile DB
- ▸ Sync DB

Information is updated based on the mapping direction (Import/Export) in the user profile.

The account name used in step 6 needs to have **Replicating Directory Changes** permission on the domain.

There's more...

To ensure that the User Profile Synchronization Service is running, follow these steps:

1. In Central Administration, click **Manage Services on server** under the section named **Service Applications**.

2. Navigate to the **User Profile Synchronization Service** as seen in the following screenshot:

User Profile Service	Started	Stop
User Profile Synchronization Service	Started	Stop

3. Click **Start**.

More info

The User Profile Service cannot utilize managed accounts.

Changing import/export for user profiles

SharePoint 2010 synchronization is a two way process—import and export. As stated in the previous recipe, import/export is mutually exclusive and must be configured at the property level.

By default, all properties are import only. This is because when the first synchronization takes place, we want to populate the profile properties in SharePoint and not Active Directory.

As users work with the system and the data matures, it makes sense that some properties should be written back to Active Directory.

This recipe shows how to change the flow (import/export) of data for one property, Picture, to go from SharePoint to Active Directory.

Getting ready

You must have farm-level administrative permissions to the Central Administration site. There must be an instance of the User Profile Service running.

How to do it...

1. Open the Central Administration screen and click **Application Management**.

2. The third section is **Service Applications**. Under this section, click **Manage service applications**.

3. Find the **User Profile Service Application** and left-click to the right of the name—the line will be highlighted. Click **Manage** on the ribbon.

4. Under the **People** section, click **Manage User Properties**.

5. Navigate to the property named **Picture**. Hover over the property until you see a drop-down list. Click the **Edit** option from the list as shown here:

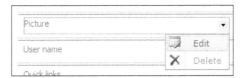

6. Navigate to the **Add New Mapping** section.

7. Click the drop-down labeled **Direction** and select **Export** from the list.

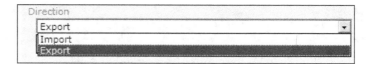

8. Click **OK**.

How it works...

Updating is a two-way process done at a granular (property) level. Utilizing the synchronization database and user profile database, the process performs the correct method based on the direction setting for the property.

In order for SharePoint to allow a user to edit a property, the **Edit Setting** property, on the edit user profile property page, must be set to allow users to update values.

There's more...

Properties must have a mapping from SharePoint, back to Business Connectivity Services or the directory.

See also

▶ *Creating a synchronization connection*

Adding a user subtype for user profile

Subtypes are a way of classifying users with a more granular set of properties. Companies have many types of users. Here are some of the types:

▶ Consultants

▶ Employees (Hourly/Salary)

▶ Interns

▶ Retired employees

This recipe will show how to create a subtype and classify someone.

Getting ready

You must have farm-level administrative permissions to the Central Administration site. The User Profile Service should be running with users from Active Directory.

How to do it...

1. Open the **Central Administration** screen and click **Application Management**.

2. The third section is **Service Applications**. Under this section, click **Manage service applications**.

3. Find **User Profile Service Application** and left-click to the right of the name— the line will be highlighted. Click **Manage** on the ribbon.

4. Under the section named **People**, click **Manage User Sub-types**.

5. The following page will be displayed:

Enter the value as **Consultant** for the **Name** as well as the **Display Name...** field.

6. Click **Create**.

How it works...

SharePoint 2010 creates everyone under the **Default User Profile Subtype**. All subtypes show up under the **Remove Existing Sub-types** section as shown in the following screenshot:

The administrator simply needs to select the subtype and click **Remove**.

There's more...

When editing a user's profile, the administrator can reclassify them by subtype. A drop-down appears at the top of the edit page. The administrator can change the subtype and then click **Save**.

A case where this may have to be applied is when a person is hired by a company on contract; such employees need to be reclassified.

Creating a new user profile property

By default, a SharePoint user profile comes with approximately 68 defined properties. The better populated these elements are, the better the integrity of the social experience in SharePoint.

Many of these properties are mapped to corresponding values in Active Directory. In this way, they can be updated in AD and then the changes are reflected in SharePoint (after a user profile synchronization).

New to SharePoint 2010 is the ability to update AD from SharePoint. While this is not the point of this recipe, it is important to have this information.

While SharePoint has many properties, there always seems to be the business use case outlining a property that SharePoint does not cover. This can be a result of the enterprise and terminology used.

A large enterprise such as a bank is the example we will use in this recipe. We will create a property to store a branch office location where the employee is located. Creating this property helps classify an employee's location at a granular level.

Functions such as audiences can be used to target content to that branch and its employees. In a fast-paced environment where employees may switch branches often, utilizing newsfeeds helps others to know where the employee is located. This provides tangible business value.

Getting ready

You must have farm-level administrative permissions to the Central Administration site.

How to do it...

1. Open the **Central Administration** screen and click **Application Management**.
2. The third section is **Service Applications**. Under this section, click **Manage service applications**.

3. Find the **User Profile Service Application** and click to the right of the name—the line will be highlighted.

4. Under the **People** section, click **Manage User Properties**.

5. Click **New Property**.

6. The following screenshot is displayed. Fill in as directed. (Due to the size of the screen, it has been separated into two parts.)

- ❑ **Name**: BranchOffice
- ❑ **Display Name**: Branch Office
- ❑ **Type**: string
- ❑ **Length**: 60
- ❑ **Sub-type of Profile**: Leave as checked
- ❑ **User Description**: Bank Branch office
- ❑ **Policy Setting:** Required
- ❑ **Default Privacy Setting**: Everyone
- ❑ **User can override**: Leave unchecked
- ❑ **Edit Settings**: Choose Do not allow users to edit values for this property

- ❑ **Display Settings**: Check all three boxes that start with Show...
- ❑ **Search Settings**: Leave the Indexed option checked

Click **OK**.

How it works...

After completing the recipe, Branch Office shows as a mandatory field in the user profile. In addition, the property is now part of the newsfeed for everyone to see. See the next screenshot from the Newsfeed section:

Custom Properties		Show To
Branch Office:	Topeka Bank Branch Office	Everyone

User profiles are saved in the user profile database. This information is collected by a timer job. Combining information from the social database, the information is collected into the user profile database for activity feeds.

The timer job User Profile Service Application – Activity Feed Job must be running (enabled) in order for this information to be populated properly in the Newsfeed.

In the example we have just seen, we did not map this field to an active directory field. This means the user profile sync will have no bearing either way (Import or Export) on this property.

There's more...

Outlook 2010 has the ability to display a SharePoint Activity feed.

10
Backup and Restore

In this chapter, we will cover:

- ▶ Recycle Bin settings in Central Administration
- ▶ Performing a site collection backup
- ▶ Exporting sites
- ▶ Importing sites
- ▶ Recovering data from an unattached content database
- ▶ Backing up a farm (multiple threads) in Central Administration
- ▶ Restoring from a backup in Central Administration

Introduction

Backup and restore are critical components when working with SharePoint. This is the information age, and for a company, its data is one of its valued assets. Hence, performing a daily backup of the SharePoint 2010 farm is good practice.

There are several environmental conditions in which a restore may be necessary:

- ▶ **Disaster Recovery** (**DR**): This is the extreme case, but we cannot anticipate when natural disasters might strike. An organization must be prepared for such disasters and have its processes and data in a separate geographical area.
- ▶ **Hardware**: Servers run for long durations and have a lot of load. Parts break and become outdated.
- ▶ **Data**: Data gets deleted and needs to be restored. It is common for users to request for data to be restored. This could be for a variety of reasons, such as data being deleted inadvertently or data that has been archived off the system. The data could be in the root site collection or buried in a subsite.

- ▸ **Viruses**: Documents are excellent carriers of viruses. Word documents are especially susceptible to virus attacks, as it is possible to embed a code that performs actions against the file system.

- ▸ **Corruption:** SharePoint has a lot of moving parts and with solutions and features, sandboxing, and customizations it is quite easy for a user (administrator or developer) to inadvertently corrupt a component of the system. A manual way of protecting against this is by limiting who can do what. This is done through governance and audits.

These items are unpredictable and uncontrollable. To gain the maximum out of SharePoint, it must be configured properly, which requires effort. It is well worth preserving that effort, and the content within SharePoint, with a great backup and DR plan.

SharePoint 2010 has taken the above into account and has a three-tier approach to backup and recovery. Refer to the following diagram:

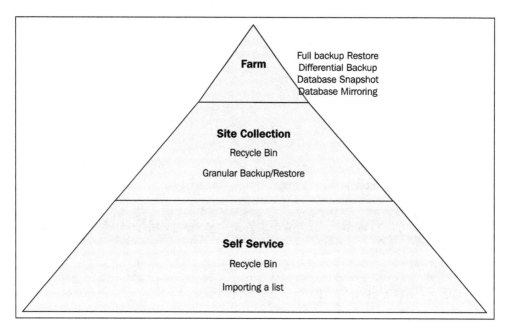

The pyramid shows different levels of empowerment, in the ecosystem of backup and recovery, in SharePoint 2010. The base of the pyramid represents the end user and the capabilities that they possess. The middle tier is the Site Collection Administrators, with a cross-over with the Farm Administrator. The top of the pyramid represents what the Farm Administrator can do in conjunction with a Database Administrator.

The following recipes are only a fundamental start to a good backup and recovery solution within SharePoint. They must be combined to complement each other. In addition, the best way to have a foolproof process is to script the backup and recovery process in PowerShell. This takes human error out of the equation.

That said, it is critical for an administrator to understand the tools they have at their disposal. These recipes will assist administrators in understanding the tools built into SharePoint.

Recycle Bin settings in Central Administration

As mentioned in the introduction, the first step in data recovery involves the first stage Recycle Bin. Anything that is deleted from a site ends up here.

When an item is deleted from the first stage Recycle Bin, it ends up in the second stage Recycle Bin. This is the **site collection Recycle Bin**.

These are simply libraries that act as containers for the discarded content. Both of these libraries are configurable.

In this recipe, we will modify the current Recycle Bin configuration of an existing web application.

Getting ready

You must have administrator privileges on the SharePoint farm.

How to do it...

1. Open **Central Administration** and click **Application Management**.
2. Click **Manage Web Applications** under the **Web Applications** section.
3. Find the web application and click to the right of the name—the line will be highlighted.
4. Click **General Settings** on the ribbon.

5. The **Web Application General Settings** page pops up. Scroll down to the **Recycle Bin** section, as seen in the following screenshot:

Recycle Bin

Specify whether the Recycle Bins of all of the sites in this web application are turned on. Turning off the Recycle Bins will empty all the Recycle Bins in the web application.

The second stage Recycle Bin stores items that end users have deleted from their Recycle Bin for easier restore if needed. Learn about configuring the Recycle Bin.

Recycle Bin Status:
  ⊙ On   ○ Off
Delete items in the Recycle Bin:
  ⊙ After [30] days
  ○ Never
Second stage Recycle Bin:
  ⊙ Add [50] percent of live site quota for second stage deleted items.
  ○ Off

6. Make sure the **After** option is selected under the **Delete items in the Recycle Bin** setting. Change the value of the **Delete items...** setting from **30 days** (default value) to **15 days**. Click **OK**.

How it works...

The Recycle Bin is a library. The first stage Recycle Bin is tied to the user. The second stage Recycle Bin is scoped at the site collection level.

This means that a Site Collection Administrator needs to be involved in order to retrieve a document from the second stage Recycle Bin. This Recycle Bin has two views:

▶ **End user Recycle Bin items**: This shows the documents deleted by users that are in their Recycle Bins.

▶ **Deleted from end user Recycle Bin**: This shows documents that are no longer in a user's Recycle Bin and are only available to the Site Collection Administrator.

There's more...

A Site Collection Administrator can view Recycle Bin items by following these steps:

1. Navigate to the site collection web page. This is the root website that was created after creation of a web application.

2. Click **Site Actions**.

3. Under the **Site Collection Administration** section, click **Recycle Bin.**

Now the administrator can either restore or delete an item, they can also empty the Recycle Bin.

More info

The quota that is set for the second stage Recycle Bin is based on the site collection, not the web application. If a site collection has no quota defined and Off is not selected in the second stage Recycle Bin, the quota is infinite.

Performing a site collection backup

The next three recipes showcase SharePoint 2010's integrated granular backup and restore capability.

One content database can contain several site collections. As the amount of data grows in an organization, the content database grows quickly, along with the value of the information in a site collection. It is the administrator's job to monitor this growth and ensure the data is backed up at regular intervals.

There is a chance that the database either grows too large or someone needs something restored from a particular site collection.

To reduce the size of the content database, the administrator can split off the information by site collection. Splitting off the information by site collection, and parsing it out to another physical content database, reduces the size of the existing content database.

The other condition entails restoring the whole content database from a backup. However, this is quite painful for every site collection in that content database—the pain of restoring to a point in time and the pain of downtime. Because of these two conditions this may not be a viable option.

The best option, as the data in a site collection matures, is to split the data from a site collection and put it into its own content database. In this recipe, a site collection will be backed up from a content database that contains more than one site collection.

Getting ready

You must have administrator privileges on the SharePoint farm. You should also have a content database that contains more than one site collection.

How to do it...

1. Open the **Central Administration** screen and click **Backup and Restore**.
2. The second section is **Granular Backup**. Under this section, click **Perform a site collection backup**.

3. The following page is displayed. Fill in the required details.

```
Readiness
  No site collection backup is in progress.
  Timer service is running.

Site Collection

Select a site collection.                          Site Collection: http://2008server:7777/sites/ts ▾

File location:                                     Filename:
Specify the destination for the backup package.    [                              ]

                                                   ☐ Overwrite existing file
                                                   Example: \\backup\SharePoint\Site1.bak
```

- **Site Collection**: Choose the name of the site collection from the drop-down list.
- **File location**: Enter a name for the file. Click the **Overwrite...** box if appropriate.

Click **OK**.

How it works...

This functionality is useful for backing up site collections and its contents. This includes lists and content, permissions, feature settings, and sites. This data is written to a file that can be used in the restore action process.

When navigating to the backup page, there is a section called **Readiness** at the top. This shows any running instances of the backup. It also shows the timer service status.

Finally, after clicking **OK**, the process navigates the user to the **Granular Backup Job Status** page. This shows anything in process, along with any previous jobs that were run and the status of these jobs.

There's more...

PowerShell can be used to back up a site collection. The following is the command:

```
backup-spsite -identity http://domain/sites/scname -path \\server\backup\
file.bak
```

More info

The Central Administration application pool account must have full access to the backup folder.

Exporting sites

SharePoint 2010 contains another component to the granular backup—the ability to export sites and lists.

The benefit of this in an administrator's toolbox is the capability of moving content at a granular level. While users have the capability of creating templates and saving data with their lists, there is a limit to the size of templates. Administrators can move this information, and can write scripts in PowerShell on what needs to be done, for maximum efficiency.

In this recipe, we will export a site under a site collection.

Getting ready

You must have administrator privileges on the SharePoint farm. There must be a site created under the site collection.

How to do it...

1. Open the **Central Administration** screen and click **Backup and Restore**.
2. The second section is **Granular Backup**. Under this section, click **Export a site or list**.
3. The following page is displayed:

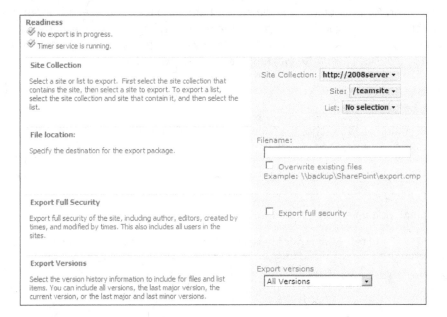

Fill in the required data.

- ❑ **Site Collection**: Select the site collection where the site is located.
- ❑ **Site**: Select the subsite from the drop-down list.
- ❑ **List**: Leave at **No selection**.
- ❑ **File location**: Enter a name for the file. Check the **Overwrite...** option if appropriate.
- ❑ **Export Full Security**: Leave this unchecked.
- ❑ **Export Versions**: Leave at **All Versions**.

Click **OK**.

How it works...

Export sites takes all the site objects including installed features, files (pages and content), lists, and all child sites and the associated content.

The administrator must choose an existing site collection and site. Leaving the **List** value at **No selection**, implies that we will be exporting all of the lists. Versions are a component of lists and have no bearing in the above recipe.

If a list is being exported, there are four options to choose from for versioning: **All Versions**, **Last Major**, **Current Version**, and **Last Minor**.

Finally, an export log is created in the directory where the backup is located. This log shows all the assets that were exported, along with the order in which they were exported. It will also show an error if we try to overwrite a file that already exists, and if the checkbox that allows the overwriting of files (**Overwrite existing files**) is not checked.

There's more...

PowerShell can be used to script the exports instead of doing them one by one in Central Administration. The command for site import is:

```
Export-SPWeb http://domain/sites/ts/teamsite -Path \\server\backup\file.
bak
```

The command for item export using PowerShell is:

```
Export-SPWeb http://domain/sites/ts/teamsite -ItemURL "Lists/
Announcements" -Path \\server\backup\file.bak
```

► _Importing sites_

Importing sites

Importing sites in SharePoint 2010 at a granular level can be accomplished only through PowerShell.

Importing is akin to restoring the assets of the site. This can also be done for an item.

This recipe shows how to restore the site from the previous recipe.

Getting ready

An export sites file must exist.

The user must have access to one of the servers running PowerShell 2.0 and the user should be a member of the `WSS_ADMIN_WPG` group on the local computer. The user must also be a member of the `db_owner` database role and `SharePoint_Shell_Access` role in the following databases:

► Source content database

► Administration content database

► Destination content database

How to do it...

1. Click on the **Start** button on the web frontend.

2. Under **All Programs**, navigate to the `Microsoft SharePoint 2010 Products` folder.

3. Right-click on **SharePoint 2010 Management Shell** and click **Run as Administrator**. The PowerShell console will appear.

4. Type the following into the console window. Once the command is entered, press the _Enter_ key.

```
Import-SPWeb http://domain/sites/ts/teamsite -Path \\server\
backup\file.bak
```

How it works...

Importing can be a bit more perilous than exporting. There are several things to be aware of:

> ▶ When importing a subsite, there must be a template that matches the one being imported. It must already be provided before trying to do an import.

> ▶ For a list, certain items can be imported. By default, the whole list is imported, and if the list exists it will be overwritten. However, by specifying –updateversions with the ignore parameter, only new items will be imported.

Just like the export, the import utility generates a log file that can be looked into if the results do not meet the expectations. This is located in the same directory as the backup.

See also

> ▶ *Exporting sites*

Recovering data from an unattached content database

One of the new tools in an administrator's toolbox is the ability to pull data from a database snapshot or from a detached content database. The pulled data is then saved in a file. The data can then be restored to a new location in a live database.

Administrators can minimize downtime and the possibility of error when pulling content from one database to another. Users can request data that may have been archived or lost through the Recycle Bin process. This data can quickly be obtained.

The biggest gain from this type of granular restore is that the content database does not need to be attached to a web application, and recovery takes place outside of the attached instance. Due to the separation of duties, the SharePoint administrator may not have access to SQL Management Studio. With this, the administrator does not need the SQL tool.

There are many ramifications of this capability in the business process. All of this is predicated on the knowledge that the content database has been backed up in some way and is archived somewhere. Capability does not replace sound backup policies and actions.

This recipe will show how to pull data into a file from an unattached content database. The information can then be imported into SharePoint via the import recipe.

Getting ready

You must have administrator privileges on the SharePoint farm. There must be one available detached database. Lastly, you need to have read permission to the unattached content database, which may be different from the Central Administrator logged in user.

How to do it...

1. Open the **Central Administration** screen and click **Backup and Restore**.
2. The second section is **Granular Backup**. Under this section, click **Recover data from an unattached content database**.
3. The following page is displayed:

Fill in the required data.

- ❑ **Database Server**: This is the name of your SQL Server instance.
- ❑ **Database Name**: This is the name of your content database.
- ❑ **SQL authentication**: Select the **Windows authentication** option.
- ❑ **Operation to Perform**: Choose the **Export site or list** option.

Click **OK**.

4. The same screen appears as was shown in the third step of the *Exporting sites* recipe. This time we will export a list item.

   ❑ **Site Collection**: Select the site collection where the site is located.

   ❑ **Site**: Select the subsite from the drop-down list.

   ❑ **Lists**: Choose the **Announcements list** option.

   ❑ **File location**: Enter a name for the file. Check the **Overwrite existing files** option if appropriate.

   ❑ **Export Full Security**: Leave this unchecked.

   ❑ **Export Versions**: Leave at **All Versions**.

   Click **OK**.

How it works...

The operation shown in this recipe works in exactly the same way as the *Export sites* recipe. The only difference is that the content database is not attached to a web application and is accessible through the browser. The other key difference being that information can be accessed from a content database snapshot.

Do not confuse unattached with detaching a database in SQL Server. This is not the same operation and this functionality will not work on a detached database.

You have the option to pick one of three ways to specify what you are recovering:

▶ **Browse Content**: This allows you to see the site collections and lists within a content database.

▶ **Backup a site collection**: Gives the option to back up a site collection.

▶ **Export site or list**: This is the same as what was shown in the **Export sites** recipe.

After the information is retrieved, use the *Import sites* recipe in order to upload the information to another content database.

There's more...

PowerShell can be used to create a snapshot of the content database. Snapshots are supported in the Enterprise version of SQL Server.

Briefly, a snapshot is a picture of the database frozen in a point of time. It is read only. Snapshots are a great help for reporting, testing, and updates. It is important to understand that a database cannot be dropped, detached, or restored when it has a snapshot.

The following commands show how to create a snapshot.

```
$spfCDB = get-spcontentdatabase wss_contentdb
$spfCDB.Snapshots.CreateSnapshot
```

See also

- ▸ *Exporting sites*
- ▸ *Importing sites*

Backing up a farm in Central Administration

Outside of keeping the farm running properly through monitoring, the other major priority for a Farm Administrator should be ensuring that there is a proper backup of the organization's farm. A SharePoint 2010 farm can consist of many components, some of which have dependencies on others.

The state service is a good example of a service application that other components rely on, whereas the user profile service is another. These components must be backed up properly, in order to have a fully functioning farm, operating with integrity, when doing a restore such as in the case of a disaster recovery.

A SharePoint 2010 administrator should know and understand what the different components are and what is installed. Only with this knowledge can they understand the ramifications of when to schedule backups and how often and which components need to be backed up more often than others.

Here are some of the SharePoint 2010 assets that should be considered in a backup plan:

- ▸ Configuration database
- ▸ Service applications
- ▸ Content databases
- ▸ Administration database
- ▸ Custom applications such as those used in the Sandbox
- ▸ Certificates used when creating trust relationships
- ▸ Data sources that are used by Business Connectivity Services (BCS)
- ▸ Form-based authentication file settings in `web.config`

This recipe shows how to do a full farm backup using Central Administration.

Getting ready

You must have administrator privileges on the SharePoint farm.

How to do it...

1. Open the **Central Administration** screen and click **Backup and Restore**.

2. The first section is **Farm Backup and Restore**. Under it, click **Perform a backup**.

3. The `backup.aspx` page is displayed with a hierarchy of components that can be backed up. The first item is the **Farm,** as shown in the following screenshot:

4. Check the box associated with **Farm**.

5. Click **Next**.

6. A new page is displayed. Fill in the required information.

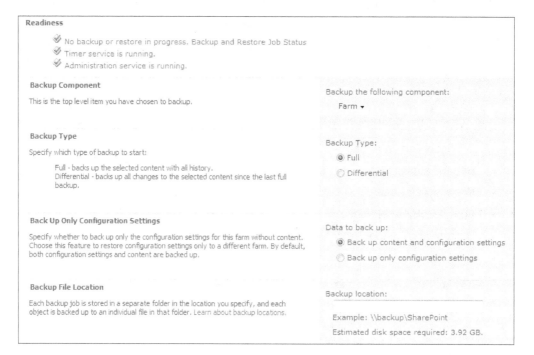

- ❑ **Backup Component**: No action is required.
- ❑ **Backup Type**: Select **Full**.
- ❑ **Back Up Only Configuration Settings**: Select **Back up content and configuration settings**.
- ❑ **Backup File Location**: Enter in a location for the backup.

7. Click **Start Backup**.

How it works...

The backup through Central Administration (as shown) initiates a SQL Server backup of content. Content is not being referred to here as just the content database, but it encompasses service application databases, the configuration database, and search assets.

In step 5, there were several parameters to the backup. The first thing is deciding between a full and a differential backup. The difference is that a differential backup stores the changes only from the last backup. A full backup is just that, everything.

The second choice is the ability to back up only the configuration settings. This backs up the configuration database. The other data choice was to back up the configuration and content. This is more likely to be the scenario that will be chosen.

When the backup is started, a running list of all the assets is kept up to date in the **Backup and Restore Job Status** page.

When the process is finished, it will indicate success or failure. Even if one content database fails and everything else succeeds, the process will report failure.

There's more...

It is important to understand that the service application and the service proxies are backed up separately, even though you may have installed a component and created a proxy such as the managed metadata service.

To back up one service at a time, select either of the checkboxes under **Shared Services**; on the other hand, to back up both together, check both the checkboxes under **Shared Services**.

☐	⊟ Shared Services	Shared Services
☐	⊞ Shared Services Applications	Shared Services Applications
☐	⊞ Shared Services Proxies	Shared Services Proxies

There may be times when you want to back up one of the service applications and its associated proxy. To do this, you must expand both Share Services Applications and Shared Services Proxies, and pick the related service application and proxy.

Furthermore, many service application databases cannot be backed up individually. To do this, a SQL Server backup must be configured and scheduled.

More info

Under the **Backup and Restore** section, there is a menu item called **Configure Backup Settings**. The following screenshot shows what the page consists of:

Number of Threads

Specify the number of threads to use for backup and restore. More threads may lead to improved performance, however, information in the log files for backup and restore may become more difficult to read.

Number of backup threads:
3
Possible Values: 1-10
Number of restore threads:
3
Possible Values: 1-10

Backup File Location

Each backup job is stored in a separate folder in the location you specify, and each object is backed up to an individual file in that folder. Learn about backup locations.

Backup location:

Example: \\backup\SharePoint

Threading is an operating system construct that represents an independent execution mechanism. The more threads the process is given, the better the performance. However, conversely the more threads, the more communication, which translates to more information in the logs.

Both backup and restore are given a default number of threads. In the preceding screenshot, both the backup as well as the restore threads stand at **3**.

The **Backup location** is the third setting that can be configured.

Restoring from a backup in Central Administration

In the last recipe, we saw how to back up the complete SharePoint 2010 farm in Central Administration.

In the event of a failure, that backup must be used to restore the farm. Another reason for a restore may be new hardware installation.

This recipe shows how to do a restore.

Getting ready

You must have administrator privileges on the SharePoint farm. A backup must have been run prior to doing this recipe.

How to do it...

1. Open the **Central Administration** screen and click **Backup and Restore**.
2. The first section is **Farm Backup and Restore**. Under it, click **Restore from a backup**.
3. The following page is displayed:

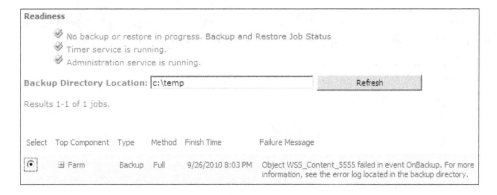

Select the backup you wish to restore.

4. A hierarchical listing of backup assets will be presented with checkboxes beside each. Check the **Farm** option to restore everything.
5. Click **Next**.

6. A detailed restore listing will be presented, which consists of five options.

   ❏ **Restore Component**: This will be **farm**.

   ❏ **Restore Only Configuration Settings**: The choice to restore configuration, or both content and configuration. Choose both.

   ❏ **Restore Options**: Click Same configuration. Click **OK** to the resulting confirmation dialog.

   ❏ **Login Names and Passwords**: You need to provide the password for the content databases and service applications.

   ❏ **New Names**: This is predicated on the Restore Options. When the **Same configuration** option is chosen, these controls are disabled.

   ❏ Click **Start Restore**.

How it works...

As the restore is running, the process status can be viewed from the **Backup and Restore Job Status** page. Timer service jobs run the restore. In the event of errors, the failure message column will enumerate the nature of the issue. If more details are needed, the `sprestore.log` file in the backup directory will further clarify the failure.

Restore works on an apples to apples basis. This means if a single server farm is being restored, it must be done from a single server backup. Likewise, a multiple server farm backup cannot be restored into a single server farm.

The service applications that are restored will not be automatically started. They must be manually started using Central Administration (**Manage Services on server**) or PowerShell.

Any trust relationships that existed must be redone.

There's more...

When restoring the farm, there are several items that must be done manually:

▸ Alternate access mapping setting must be recreated

▸ External data sources, used by BCS, must be reconfigured

▸ Proxy groups must be reconfigured to have a correct association with the service application proxies

▸ Web application must be configured with the proxy groups

More info

PowerShell can be used to perform the restore. It must be done with the Farm account's credentials, using the following command:

```
Restore-SPFarm -Directory <BackupFolder> -RestoreMethod Overwrite
[-BackupId <GUID>]
```

11
Performance Monitoring

In this chapter, we will cover:

- ▸ Enabling HTTP Request Monitoring and Throttling
- ▸ Using SQL Profiler
- ▸ What and how to monitor with Performance Monitor
- ▸ Implementing Visual Round Trip Analyzer

Introduction

Performance and monitoring is all about being proactive, and providing a healthy (free from viruses, enough storage space, proper server utilization, and so on), efficiently working SharePoint 2010 site for users. Sites may function, but an administrator must be cognizant enough to determine whether or not they are working efficiently and whether they can be scaled. To answer these questions, the administrator needs to be aware of the tools at his/her disposal.

SharePoint is a broad and deep application, having hundreds of different technologies built into it. Add to this the capability to integrate with existing technologies. The result of all this is a complex application that can efficiently resolve user issues but is challenging to monitor.

Let's take an example of the **Content Query Web Part** (**CQWP**). It is a great technology for exposing content on the home page from other parts of the site. Often, important content is buried across sites or deep within a site. Users have to navigate through too many clicks to find the information.

The obvious place to put the CQWP is on the home page. One day, the administrator gets reports from users of the page hosting this web part having performance issues; users report page timeouts to the administrator and they report strange information on the page.

The administrator must go through a list of possible causes. The causes might include:

- Is the problem how many sites CQWP traverses to display data?
- Has the CQWP been customized to bring custom fields back?
- Does the CQWP bring back only the fields that were specified?
- Was a custom query written using CAML and put into the CQWP? If so, how efficient is that query?
- Were there any overrides, and if yes, what were they and how can they affect performance?
- How many CQWPs are being used on one page?

The point being made here is that this is an out of the box web part and there is a lot that a user can do with it that can affect page load time.

Server-side code introduces a different complexity, such as the possibility of memory leaks. Memory leaks in a system are like termites—you don't notice them at first, but when you do, your system seems out of resources. Like termites, identifying and getting rid of system leaks is a major pain point and cannot be easily done.

SharePoint has a best practice analyzer included with Central Administration, which has been covered in *Chapter 5*, *Monitoring and Reporting*, under the recipe named *Editing rule definitions in health analyzer*. This is powerful and extensible and provides critical information to the administrator on the health of the farm.

But just like the carpenter who could build a house with just a hammer, there are other powerful tools that supplement the health analyzer. These tools are found outside of SharePoint and help the administrator to perform his/her duties more efficiently. The tools will point to other possible issues such as memory leaks and page load times that affect SharePoint. This gives you, as an administrator, a broad picture of the possible issues.

Once these issues are identified, there should be possible resolutions. One such tool featured in the recipes here does just that. The tool is named Virtual Round Trip Analyzer. It provides the suggested best practices.

These tools should be used carefully and in conjunction with each other. Becoming knowledgeable on what is available and how to utilize them will arm you with the information you need, making you a smart SharePoint 2010 administrator.

Enabling HTTP Request Monitoring and Throttling

To understand resources and the SharePoint 2010 application, the analogy of a state government will be used. A state government provides the foundation for a system of governance, checks and balances, and branches to that government at a local and regional level. The government and its branches provide infrastructure and resources to the citizens.

Citizens are the users of this infrastructure. Citizens create businesses and provide more resources, but at the same time also use the resources provided by the government. With an increased number of users and businesses, the stress on the government and its infrastructure grows. The government must scale its resources and performance to meet the needs of its users.

This is SharePoint 2010—a super .NET application that provides resources and an infrastructure to its users and businesses. Resources are critical to the health and performance of this ecosystem.

As an administrator, it is critical to understand the resources consumed by SharePoint 2010. In SharePoint, it is possible to manage these resources and put limits in place, so the servers remain healthy and do not go down.

This recipe shows how to enable HTTP Request Monitoring and Throttling.

Getting ready

You must have farm-level administrative permissions to the Central Administration site.

This recipe uses PowerShell. You must be a member of the `SharePoint_Shell_Access` database role on the configuration database. You also must be a member of the `WSS_ADMIN_WPG` local group.

How to do it...

1. Open the **Central Administration** screen and click **Application Management**.
2. The first section is **Web Applications**. Under it, click **Manage Web Applications**.
3. Click to the right of the web application so that the line is selected.
4. On the ribbon, select **General Settings** and then **Resource Throttling**.

5. At the bottom of the ensuing pop-up screen, there is a section as shown in the following screenshot:

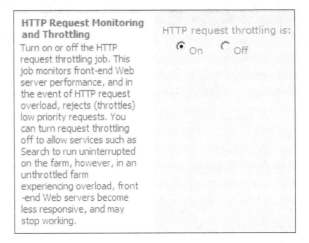

Select the **On** option.

6. Click **OK**.

7. On the publishing farm server, select click **Start | All Programs | Microsoft SharePoint 2010 Products | SharePoint 2010 Management Shell**.

8. In the PowerShell command prompt, type in the following commands:

```
$setting = (Get-SPWebApplication "http://server").
HttpthrottleSettings

$settings
```

The output of the command is shown in the following screenshot:

```
RefreshInterval             : 5000
NumberOfSamples             : 12
ThrottleClassifiers         : {SPSearchCrawlingRequestClassifier      FirstStage
                              }
PerformanceMonitors         : {Category:Memory      Counter:Available Mbytes      I
                              nstance:
                              , Category:ASP.NET      Counter:Requests Queued
                              Instance:
                              , Category:ASP.NET      Counter:Request Wait Time
                              Instance:
                              }
PerformThrottle             : True
Name                        :
TypeName                    : Microsoft.SharePoint.Utilities.SPHttpThrottleSett
                              ings
DisplayName                 :
Id                          : 384aac3f-996a-4be3-b8ed-589a211c5a68
Status                      : Online
Parent                      : SPWebApplication Name=SharePoint - 80
Version                     : 419076
Properties                  : {}
Farm                        : SPFarm Name=PZS_Config
UpgradedPersistedProperties : {}
```

How it works...

When Request Throttling is enabled, the state of each web frontend server is evaluated at a request level. A request is the information asked for on the web frontend by the user and then sent to SQL Server.

Throttling is enabled at a web application level, as shown in steps 1 to 6. Several metrics are sampled and a server health score of 0 to 10 is assigned to the request. The higher the score, the worse the state of the server.

Throttling is implemented when the score is 10. At this point, any new web page will result in a 503 error. Administrators know the 503 error page indicates that the servers have no more resources to satisfy the request.

Steps 7 and 8 show how to access the SPHttpthrottleSettings object. This is where the settings for throttling are set.

The settings are as follows:

- **RefreshInterval**: Amount of time between samples. The preceding screenshot shows the time set to five seconds (**5000** miliseconds).
- **NumberOfSample**: Samples of each counter are collected for measurement. These are weighted and used in an algorithm that cannot be modified. The default is twelve samples per minute.
- **ThrottleClassifiers**: Set of rules that classify requests.
- **PerformanceMonitors**: Specifies the counters associated with HTTP Request Monitoring and Throttling.
- **PerformThrottle**: This turns on or off request throttling for the web application specified. Display true for enabled.

There's more...

With PowerShell, you can see as well as set the performance counters that SharePoint is currently utilizing.

Use the following command to see the Throttling settings:

```
Get-SPWebApplicationHttpThrottlingMonitors http://yourserver
```

Use the following command to set the Throttling settings:

```
Set-SPWebApplicationHttpThrottlingMonitors-URL <http://yourserver>
```

More info

Thresholds cannot be configured through Central Administration. They must be configured through PowerShell. In order to read diagnostics, refer to the ULS Log and event logs located on the server.

See also

The *Editing rule definitions in health analyzer* recipe from *Chapter 5, Monitoring and Reporting*

Using SQL Profiler

SQL Profiler is not necessarily a SharePoint Administrator's tool. It is associated with the Database Administrator. However, due to SharePoint's reliance on SQL Server, it is important that an administrator understand the tool and its use.

SQL Profiler is a tool that captures every event going to SQL and saves the information in a trace file. Using the built-in recorder, the administrator can capture information and then stop when enough has been collected.

This information can be critical to debugging and performance tuning. With SQL Profiler, you can monitor SQL statements and stored procedures, slow performance, and audit and review activities.

This recipe shows how to instantiate SQL Profiler against SharePoint 2010.

Getting ready

You must have administrator permissions to connect to a specific instance of SQL Server and have permissions to execute Profiler stored procedures. You must have SQL Server Client Tools loaded to your machine.

How to do it...

1. Select **Start | All Programs | Microsoft SQL Server 2008**.
2. Select **Performance Tools | SQL Server Profiler**.
3. Select **File | New Trace**.
4. Select the server name and click **Connect**.
5. The following dialog appears:

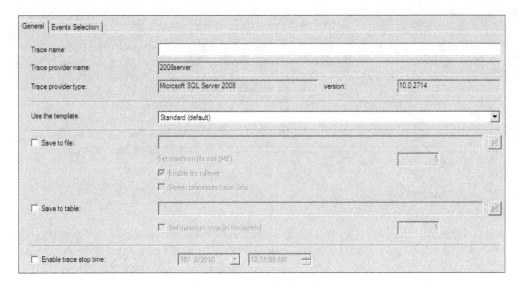

Fill in the required information.

- ❑ **Trace Name: SPTrace**.
- ❑ **Use the template**: Leave it to the default value: **Standard**.
- ❑ **Save to file**: Check this box. A filename automatically appears; save this location.

6. Click **Run**.

7. Add a list item to a list in your SharePoint team site.

8. Click on the **Stop Selected Trace** button ▪ on the menu.

How it works...

SQL Profiler attaches to an instance of your database. It can then interrogate and report on every event that takes place in that database. We need to be aware that Profiler will show activity on all the databases, which includes everything from the social databases to managed metadata to search—a lot of information to collect.

When you first clicked **Run** in the sixth step, the trace began immediately. You may have noticed how much communication there was between SharePoint 2010 and the SQL Server; even the shortest of traces produces voluminous data.

Here is a sample statement related to a particular timer job:

```
exec dbo.proc_CompleteTimerRunningJob @ServiceId='168D1873-BC36-
4E51-AF85-8E1C7162C389',@VirtualServerId='AA272A38-214B-4CE3-8F71-
2FC2BC670E7E',@JobId='A6EBD258-6575-45B4-AFB2-A6038345974F',@
ServerId='C17285C9-27C8-4C88-A989-86B5DFDDA25B',@Status=2,@
RequestGuid='9D6166F7-81F7-4813-B3EC-16581C6EBD6B'
```

It shows the timer job being completed. If the GUID were translated, we would have some powerful information at our disposal, which otherwise may not be possible through Central Administration.

There's more...

There is a second tab called Events, on the definition of a trace shown in step 5 of this recipe. An event is an action generated by SQL Server. Each event is part of a category. By leveraging templates, certain events such as locks and permissions can be grouped. This presents, in a simplified way, the data we have been tracing.

What and how to monitor with Performance Monitor

SharePoint 2010 runs on a server with Windows 2008. This has a built-in tool called Performance Monitor. As a SharePoint Administrator, you should be aware of this tool and its components.

Performance Monitor is a tool intended for use by IT professionals or computer administrators. There are many components that could limit the performance of your SharePoint system, including

- Amount of memory (RAM)
- Physical hard disks
- Processor speed
- Network
- Virtual image and the architecture around it

Performance Monitor gives a graphical representation of the measures that are chosen. This provides you with a quick way to identify problems and the trends.

In this recipe, we will show how to use Performance Monitor and change a few of the available counters.

Getting ready

To create data collector sets, configure logs, or view reports, the console must run as a member of the Administrators group or the Performance Log Users group.

How to do it...

1. Select **Start | Administrative Tools** and then select **Performance Monitor**.

2. Select the computer from the drop-down list.

3. Click the green plus sign (shown in the screenshot), which is the icon for the **Add Counters** option.

4. The **Add Counters** dialog box opens. Navigate to **Memory**, click the plus sign, and select **% Committed Bytes In Use**. Click the **Add** button below the text boxes. Your screen should look like the following screenshot:

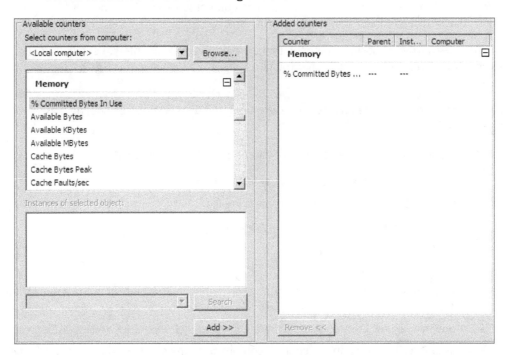

5. Follow the same process as step 3 for the following counters:

   ❏ **ASP.NET Application: Request Rejected, Requests Timed Out**

   ❏ **SharePoint Disk-Based Cache: Total blob disk size**

You should see a screen similar to the following screenshot:

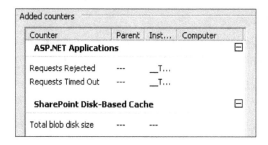

6. Click **OK**.

How it works...

Performance Monitor shows specific performance counters in a graphical view. It works in real time so that you can monitor the health of your servers.

As can be seen when choosing a counter, there are hundreds of counters. Each counter is assigned a different color and with that you can delineate which line in the graph represents which counter.

The counters can be selected not only one at a time, but also by group by holding down the *Ctrl* key.

The ribbon toolbar shown in the screenshot can be used for the following:

▸ **View Current Activity**: Real-time view of counters.

▸ **View Log Data**: Enables user to create a log file.

▸ **Change Graph Type**: Three different types: Line, Histogram, or Report.

▸ **Add**: Adds counters.

▸ **Delete**: Removes counters.

▸ **Highlight**: Click on a counter and then click highlight. This highlights the counter. It is a useful setting for focusing on a particular measure.

▸ **Copy Properties**: Creates a copy of the current selected counter and its properties.

▸ **Paste Counter List**: Imports counter settings from the clipboard. This is helpful when you have more than one server that is being monitored.

▸ **Properties**: Shows a dialog that enables the user to change the color of a line, scale, width, and style, along with adding and removing of counters. In addition, things such as the graph can be changed in a multitude of ways.

▸ **Freeze the display**: Conversely, you can then update the display or enable it in real-time again.

There's more...

If you have to go and select counters each time you need to run Performance Monitor, it is an indication of inefficient functioning. For your server instance, through trial, you will find the set of counters that give you the information you need.

Windows 2008 has the ability to create a Data Collector Set. This is a group of counters that you have defined and saved.

In Performance Monitor, on the left-hand side, there is a console tree that looks like the following screenshot:

Right-click on the **User Defined** option under **Data Collector Sets**. Click **New** and a wizard guides you to create a collection of counters.

Once the collection is created, the Data Collector Set will be shown under the **User Defined** option. By right-clicking on it, you can select the **Start** option and begin the monitoring task.

More info

Microsoft has created many performance counters. As you navigate through the list, you will see the counters related to SharePoint, FAST (if installed), and WSS.

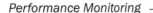

If the organization has the enterprise version of SharePoint, there are counters for the following services:

- ▶ Access Services
- ▶ PerformancePoint Services
- ▶ Excel Services
- ▶ Visio Services

These services are cache based due to their nature. If you are running any of these, monitoring them for performance tuning is advisable.

Implementing Visual Round Trip Analyzer

Visual Round Trip Analyzer (**VRTA**) is a tool that helps the SharePoint Administrator identify what is being downloaded at a web page level. One of the biggest complaints from users is the response time. This feedback always finds its way back to the administrator of the SharePoint farm.

VRTA excels in showing the network round trip relationship between the client and the server. This is also critical to the well-being of a farm. While an administrator can optimize the server response, there are several other parties that can inadvertently be working against this:

- ▶ **Web developers**: These folks create the HTML, CSS, and stylesheets.
- ▶ **End users**: They load content such as images, which directly hampers performance.
- ▶ **Application developers**: These folks load JavaScript, jQuery, and now have the client object model at their disposal.

All of these listed parties create solutions using SharePoint Designer, Notepad, and possibly Visual Studio, and the administrator would have no knowledge of this. But in the end, the administrator is the person who will get the support call.

Using VRTA, the administrator can identify the bottlenecks and involve the right parties.

This recipe shows how to run VRTA against SharePoint 2010.

Getting ready

You must have VRTA loaded on a PC (free download from the Microsoft Download Center). Netmon 3.4, also a free download, needs to be loaded on the PC. These tools should not be run on servers but on local machines. No special permissions are needed and it can be run against a public site.

How to do it...

1. Select **Start | Microsoft Visual Round Trip Analyzer**.

2. In the drop-down next to **Select Network**, ensure that the proper network is selected.

3. Open the browser and set the address to `about:blank`.

4. Click the green play button on VRTA.

5. In the browser address, type `www.sharepoint.com`.

6. Navigate to the menu item.

7. In VRTA, click the red circle.

8. Click the **All Files** tab in VRTA. You should get a screen similar to the next screenshot:

How it works...

VRTA uses Microsoft Network Monitor 3.4 packet analyzer as its foundation. Visually, it shows files and packets, along with the round trip information that occurs between a client and server.

When evaluating page loads, several factors should be taken into account:

- Distance: The round trip
- Number of round trips

> ▸ Images on a home page

> ▸ Files that need to be downloaded (CSS, JavaScript, and so on)

Using the four tabs, Main Chart, Statistics, All Files, and Analysis, the data the page is retrieving and loading can be seen in detail. In the preceding screenshot, every file that is loaded shows how long to load, the port, the type of file, a status code, and size.

Armed with this information, the administrator can observe the assets that are being used and be able to offer recommendations such as creating a sprite instead of loading each individual image, or combining JavaScript files. Hovering over each detail item will present further detail on the individual asset.

VRTA also has an Analysis tab that acts as a best practice guide. It grades the files and page on several basic factors such as an average file size rule, white spaces rule, and image clustering rule. Using a color-coded scheme, it makes recommendations to help you improve performance.

Finally, every time a recording is made, it is saved in a directory by default, whose path can be seen in the title of the VRTA application.

There's more...

The reason to start with `about:blank` is that IE will reload the page automatically and won't use cache. This will give you a real representation of your SharePoint 2010 application.

Index

S

SalesContractCT **114**
sample term **211**
Sandbox functionality
   about 99
   configuring 97, 98
SAPGFinancial group option **50**
search query
   viewing 159, 160
Search Server Express 2010 **143**
search service
   about 143
   components 144
   crawl database, adding 154-157
   crawl reports, viewing 159, 160
   Fast Search Server 2010 144
   host distribution rule, adding 157-159
   managing 146-148
   new content account 149
   property database, adding 152, 153
   query component, adding 149-151
   refinement pane, customizing 161-165
   search query, viewing 159, 160
   Search Server Express 2010 143
   setting up 144-146
   SharePoint Search Server 2010 144
search service, components
   crawler (indexer) 144
   property database 144
   query server 144
secure store service
   creating 41-43
security policy reports
   accessing 177, 178
Security Token Service (STS) certificate **68**
Send To connections. *See* multiple Send To
     connections
service
   application associations, managing 49-51
   custom security, creating 44-47
   custom service application proxy group
     creating 47-49
   deleting 39
   Excel services, setting up 51-55
   farms service, consuming 72-74

Managed Metadata Service (MMS), setting up
   63-66
Manage Service Application page 40
managing 37-40
PerformancePoint services, setting up 56-60
secure store service, creating 41, 43
SharePoint Service
publishing 69-71
Visio services, setting up 60, 62
service application associations
   managing 49-51
Set-SPUser command **169**
Shared Service Provider (SSP) **35, 36**
SharePoint 2010
   about 8, 125, 126
   activity feed, viewing 216-218
   advanced routing (content organizer), config-
     uring 180-185
   Alternate Access Mapping (AAM), creating 29,
     30
   backup and recovery solution 235
   content database, configuring 26, 28
   content deployment, configuring 188-190
   content type hub, adding 192-195
   correlation IDs, troubleshooting with 137,
     138
   current installation upgradeability, checking
     8-11
   Developer Dashboard, enabling 139-141
   documents, routing to another site 185-187
   export for user profiles, changing 225, 226
   external content types, managing 195-198
   import for user profiles, changing 225, 226
   in place records management 203-206
   lockdown mode, setting for publishing sites
     174, 175
   logging database 128-130
   logging database, accessing 126-128
   MOSS 2007, upgrading errors 17
   MOSS 2007, upgrading to SharePoint 2010
     11-16
   note associated with page, deleting 214, 215
   permission UI, checking 172, 173
   PowerShell permissions, delegating 170-172
   rule definitions in health analyzer, editing
     130-133

About Packt Publishing

Packt, pronounced 'packed', published its first book "*Mastering phpMyAdmin for Effective MySQL Management*" in April 2004 and subsequently continued to specialize in publishing highly focused books on specific technologies and solutions.

Our books and publications share the experiences of your fellow IT professionals in adapting and customizing today's systems, applications, and frameworks. Our solution-based books give you the knowledge and power to customize the software and technologies you're using to get the job done. Packt books are more specific and less general than the IT books you have seen in the past. Our unique business model allows us to bring you more focused information, giving you more of what you need to know, and less of what you don't.

Packt is a modern, yet unique publishing company, which focuses on producing quality, cutting-edge books for communities of developers, administrators, and newbies alike. For more information, please visit our website: www.PacktPub.com.

About Packt Enterprise

In 2010, Packt launched two new brands, Packt Enterprise and Packt Open Source, in order to continue its focus on specialization. This book is part of the Packt Enterprise brand, home to books published on enterprise software – software created by major vendors, including (but not limited to) IBM, Microsoft and Oracle, often for use in other corporations. Its titles will offer information relevant to a range of users of this software, including administrators, developers, architects, and end users.

Writing for Packt

We welcome all inquiries from people who are interested in authoring. Book proposals should be sent to author@packtpub.com. If your book idea is still at an early stage and you would like to discuss it first before writing a formal book proposal, contact us; one of our commissioning editors will get in touch with you.

We're not just looking for published authors; if you have strong technical skills but no writing experience, our experienced editors can help you develop a writing career, or simply get some additional reward for your expertise.

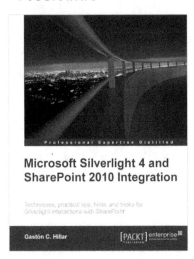

Microsoft Silverlight 4 and SharePoint 2010 Integration

ISBN: 978-1-849680-06-6   Paperback: 336 pages

Techniques, practical tips, hints, and tricks for Silverlight interactions with SharePoint

1. Develop Silverlight RIAs that interact with SharePoint 2010 data and services

2. Explore the diverse alternatives for hosting a Silverlight RIA in a SharePoint 2010 Page

3. Work with the new SharePoint Silverlight Client Object Model to interact with elements in a SharePoint Site

SharePoint Designer Tutorial: Working with SharePoint Websites

ISBN: 978-1-847194-42-8   Paperback: 188 pages

Get started with SharePoint Designer and learn to put together a business website with SharePoint

1. Become comfortable in the SharePoint Designer environment

2. Learn about SharePoint Designer features as you create a SharePoint website

3. Step-by-step instructions and careful explanations

Please check **www.PacktPub.com** for information on our titles

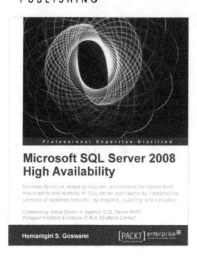

Microsoft SQL Server 2008 High Availability

ISBN: 978-1-84968-1-22-3   Paperback: 300 pages

Minimize downtime, speed up recovery, and achieve the highest level of availability and reliability for SQL server applications by mastering the concepts of database mirroring,log shipping,clustering, and replication

1.   Install various SQL Server High Availability options in a step-by-step manner

2.   A guide to SQL Server High Availability for DBA aspirants, proficient developers and system administrators

3.   Tips to enhance performance with SQL Server High Availability

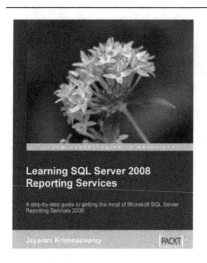

Learning SQL Server 2008 Reporting Services

ISBN: 978-1-847196-18-7   Paperback: 512 pages

A step-by-step guide to getting the most of Microsoft SQL Server Reporting Services 2008

1.   Everything you need to create and deliver data-rich reports with SQL Server 2008 Reporting Services as quickly as possible

2.   Packed with hands-on-examples to learn and improve your skills

3.   Connect and report from databases, spreadsheets, XML Data, and more

4.   No experience of SQL Server Reporting Services required

Please check **www.PacktPub.com** for information on our titles

www.ingramcontent.com/pod-product-compliance
Lightning Source LLC
LaVergne TN
LVHW062309060326
832902LV00013B/2123

* 9 7 8 1 8 4 9 6 8 1 0 8 7 *